The Country Guitar
BIG BOOK

AUTHENTIC
GUITAR TAB
EDITION

ISBN-10: 0-7692-9114-7
ISBN-13: 978-0-7692-9114-7

CONTENTS

ARTIST INDEX

SEVEN SPANISH ANGELS

Words and Music by
EDDIE SETSER and
TROY SEALS

Chorus:

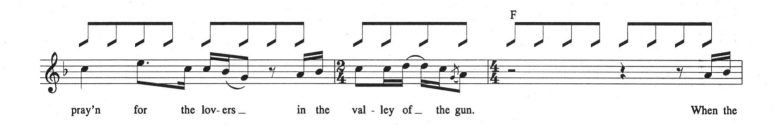

sev-en Span-ish an-gels _ at the al-tar of _ the sun.   They were

pray'n for the lov-ers _ in the val-ley of _ the gun.   When the

bat-tle stopped, and the smoke cleared, _ there was thun-der from _ the throne, _   and

2nd time to Coda

sev-en Span-ish an-gels _ took a-noth-er an-gel home. _

Verse 2: (Willie Nelson)

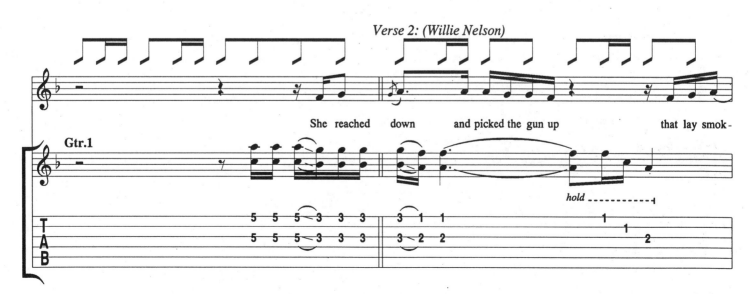

She reached down   and picked the gun up   that lay smok-

6

Seven Spanish Angels - 4 - 3

OH, PRETTY WOMAN

Words and Music by
ROY ORBISON and
BILL DEES

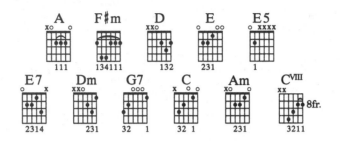

Oh, Pretty Woman - 3 - 1

10

Verse 2:
Pretty woman, don't walk on by.
Pretty woman, don't make my cry.
Pretty woman, don't walk away.
(To Coda)

A BAD GOODBYE

**Words and Music by
CLINT BLACK**

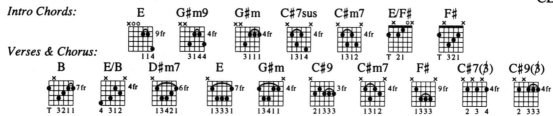

A Bad Goodbye – 3 – 1

12

Verse 2:
I'm still bound to leave you,
I surely don't know how.
My heart won't let me put you through
What my mind said should happen now.
I don't know where we'll go from here.
There may be nowhere to fly.
And the cloud I'm in just makes it all too clear
That I can't leave you with a bad goodbye.
(To Chorus:)

A Bad Goodbye – 3 – 3

LET IT BE ME

Music by
GILBERT BECAUD
English Words by
MANN CURTIS
French Words by
PIERRE DELANOE

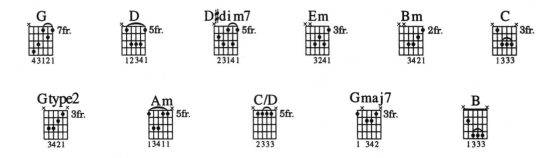

Moderately slow ♩ = 84

Intro:

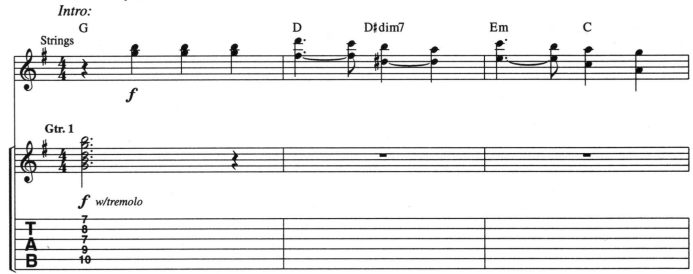

Verse 1:
Rhy. Fig. 1

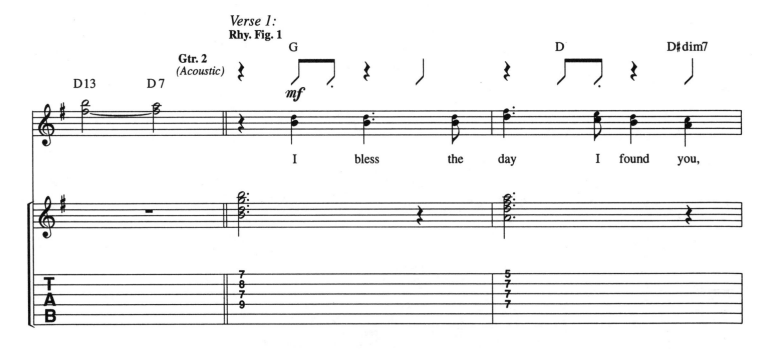

I bless the day I found you,

* Bass plays D.

cling   to some - one.   Now___ and   for - ev - er,

Bridge:
Gtr. 2

let___ it   be   me.   Each___ time   we___

meet,   love,___   I find___ com - plete   love.___

* Bass plays B.

D.S. % al Coda

Coda

Gtr. 2 tacet

Freely

rit.

hold _ |

With- out your sweet love, what would life

_ be? _ be? let _ it be me.

Verses 3 & 4:
So never leave me lonely,
Tell me you love me only
And that you'll always
Let it be me.
(To Bridge:)

Let It Be Me - 4 - 4

The Country Guitar

BIG

BOOK

A BETTER MAN

Words and Music by
CLINT BLACK and
HAYDEN NICHOLAS

Moderately ♩ = 160

Intro:

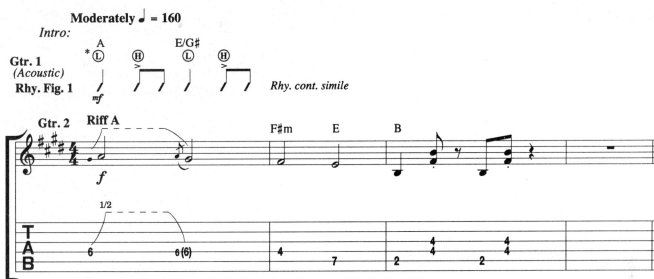

*Chords are broken between ⓛ (low strings) and ⓗ (high strings); allow all notes to ring together.

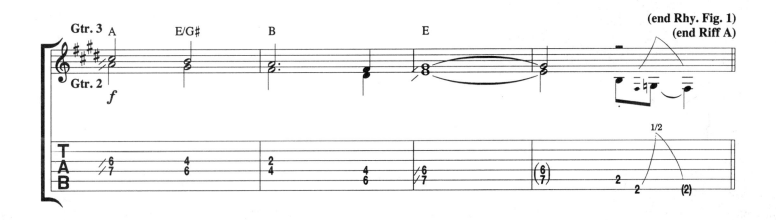

Verse:

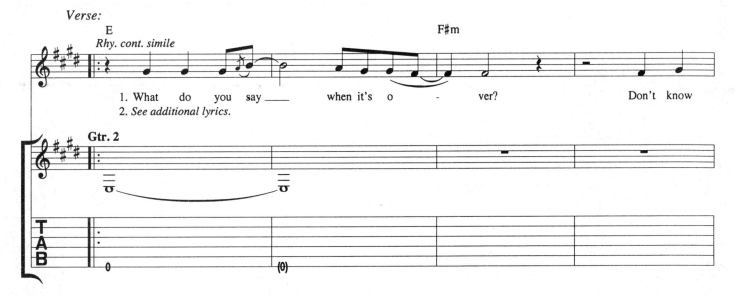

1. What do you say ___ when it's o - ver? Don't know
2. *See additional lyrics.*

if I should say ___ an-y-thing at all. ___

One day we're roll-in' in ___ the clo - ver,

next thing you know ___ we take ___ the fall. ___

2. Still, I

1. I know I'm
2. Still I'm

A Better Man – 5 – 3

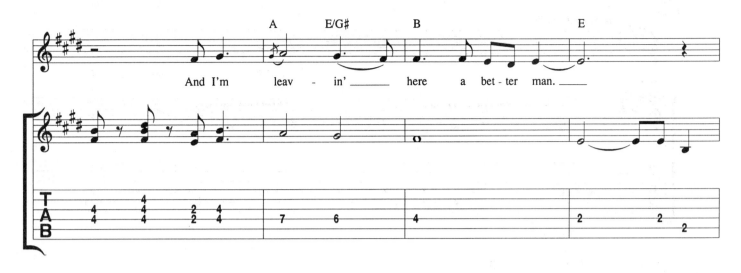

And I'm leav - in' _____ here a bet - ter man. ____

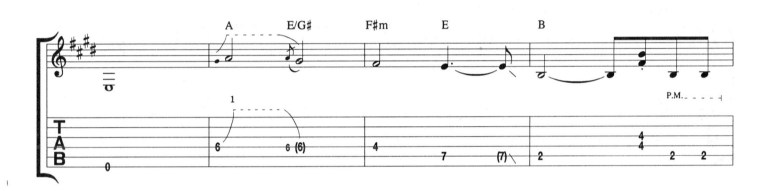

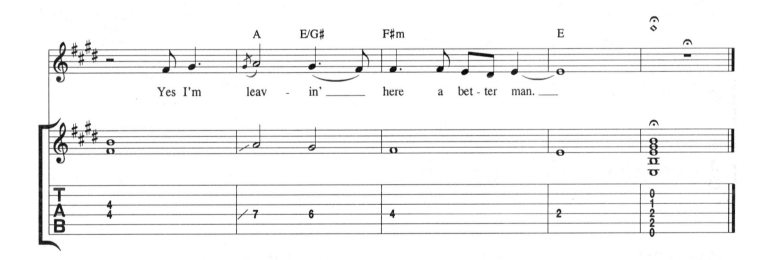

Yes I'm leav - in' _____ here a bet - ter man. ____

Verse 2:

Still, I think about the years since I first met you,
And the way it might have been without you here.
I don't know if words from me
Can still upset you, but I've just
Got to make this memory stand clear.

(To Chorus:)

Verse 3:

Guess I always knew I couldn't hold you,
But I'd never be the one to set you free.
Just like some old nursery rhyme your mama told you,
You still believe in some old meant-to-be.

(To Chorus:)

BLUE BAYOU

Words and Music by
ROY ORBISON and JOE MELSON

Verse 1:

feel so bad, ___ I've got a wor - ried mind.   I'm so lone-some   all the time.

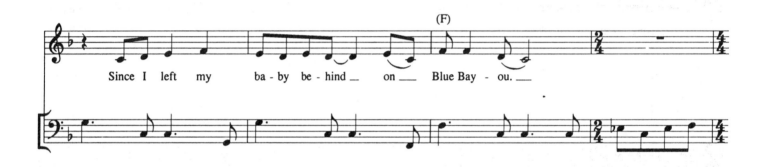

Since I left my ba - by be - hind ___ on ___ Blue Bay - ou. ___

Verses 2 & 3:

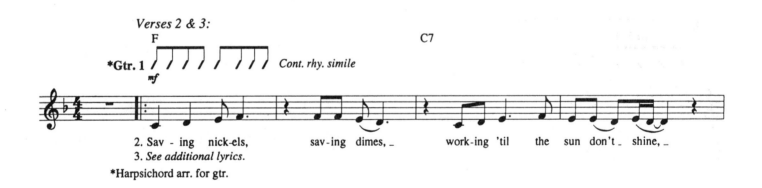

*Gtr. 1   *Cont. rhy. simile*

2. Sav - ing nick - els,   sav - ing dimes, ___   work - ing 'til the sun don't ___ shine, ___
3. *See additional lyrics.*

*Harpsichord arr. for gtr.

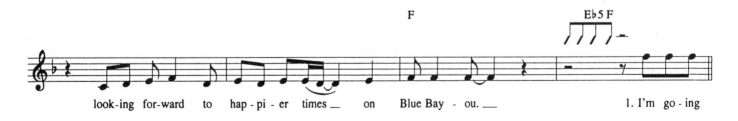

look - ing for - ward to hap - pi - er times ___ on Blue Bay - ou. ___   1. I'm go - ing

Blue Bayou - 2 - 1

Verse 3:
Oh, to see my baby again,
And to be with some of my friends.
Maybe I'd be happy then on Blue Bayou.
(To Chorus:)

Chorus 2:
I'm going back some day, gonna stay on Blue Bayou,
Where the folks are fine, and the world is mine on Blue Bayou.
Oh, that girl of mine by my side, the silver moon and the evening tide.
Oh, some sweet day, gonna take away this hurtin' inside.
I'll never be blue, my dreams come true on Blue Bayou.

BURN ONE DOWN

Words and Music by
CLINT BLACK, HAYDEN NICHOLAS
and FRANKIE MILLER

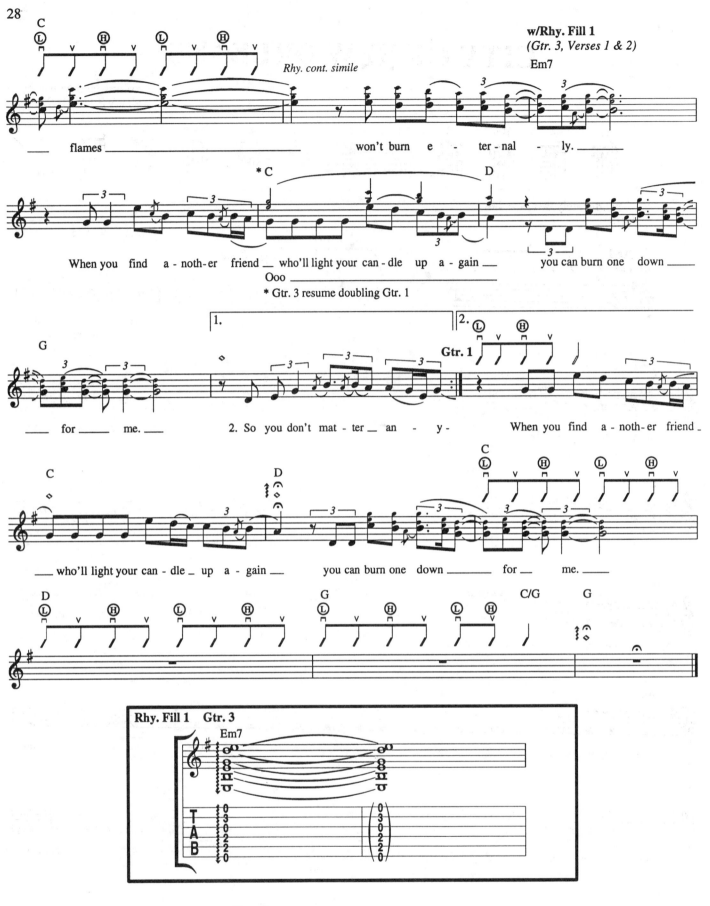

Verse 2:

So you don't matter anymore.
I'll convince myself, I'm sure.
As if I give a damn,
That's just the way I am.
So go on and pour yourself some wine
With who'll ever spend your time.
'Cause anyone can see you won't be crying over me
And you never were that kind.

(To Chorus:)

CITY OF NEW ORLEANS

Words and Music by
STEVE GOODMAN

-ed au - to - mo - biles. ___ Good morn - in' A - mer - i - ca how _ are you? _

___ Say, don't you know _ me, _ I'm your na - tive son. ___

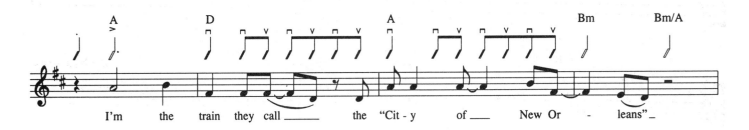

I'm the train they call ___ the "Cit - y of ___ New Or - leans" _

To Coda ⊕

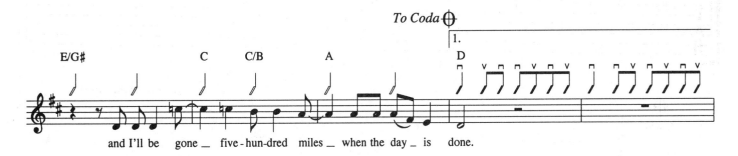

1.

and I'll be gone _ five - hun - dred miles _ when the day _ is done.

2.

2. Deal - in' done.

Guitar Solo:

(Cont. rhy. simile)

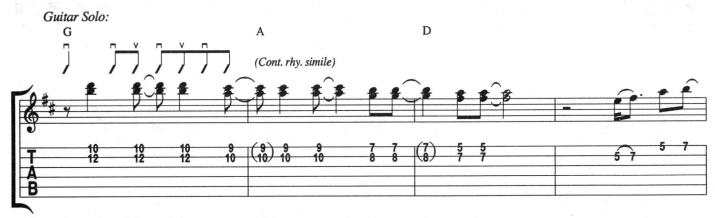

Verse 2:

Dealin' cards with the old man in the club car.
Penny a point, ain't no one keepin' score.
Pass the paper bag that holds the bottle,
Feel the wheels rumblin' 'neath the floor.
And the sons of pullman porters and the sons of engineers
Ride their father's magic carpet made of steel.
Mothers with their babes asleep rockin' to the gentle beat
And the rhythm of the rails is all they feel.

Verse 3:

Night time on the City of New Orleans,
Changin' cars in Memphis, Tennessee.
Halfway home, we'll be there by morning;
Through the Mississippi darkness rollin' down to the sea.
But all the towns and people seem to fade into a bad dream
And the steel rails still ain't heard the news.
The conductor sings his songs again,
"The passengers will please refrain,..."
This train has got the disappearing railroad blues.

CHATTAHOOCHEE

Words and Music by
ALAN JACKSON and JIM McBRIDE

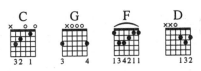

Chattahoochee – 6 – 1

Pre-Chorus:

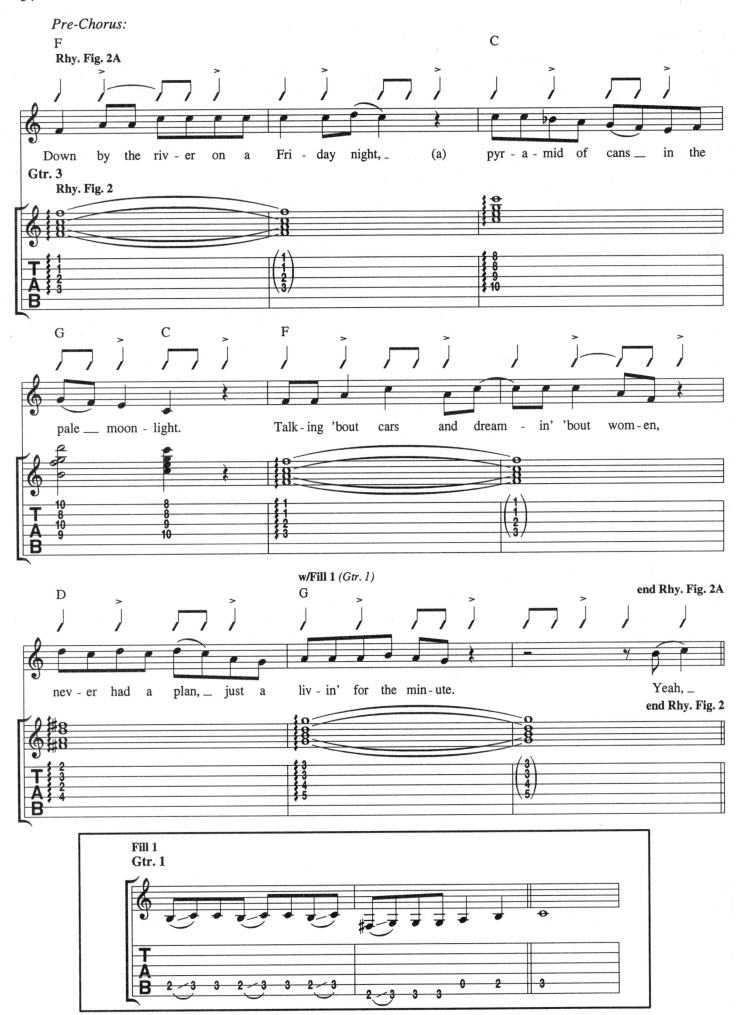

Chorus:

way down yon - der on the Chat - ta - hoo - chee, nev - er knew how much that mud - dy wa - ter

meant to me. But I learned how to swim _ and I learned who I was. _ A

To Coda ⊕

1.
lot a - bout liv - in' and a lit - tle 'bout love.

2.
lit - tle 'bout love.

Guitar Solo:

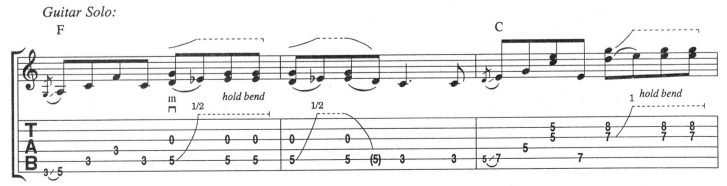

Chattahoochee – 6 – 4

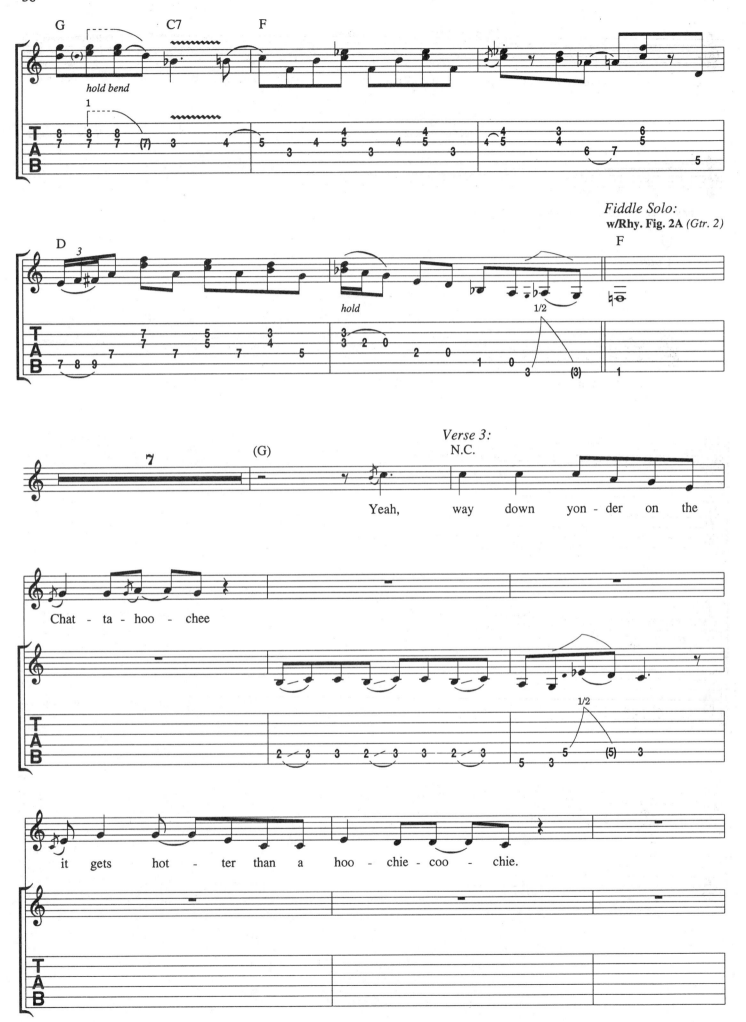

Fiddle Solo:
w/Rhy. Fig. 2A *(Gtr. 2)*

Verse 3:
N.C.

Yeah,   way   down   yon - der   on   the

Chat - ta - hoo - chee

it   gets   hot - ter   than   a   hoo - chie - coo - chie.

We laid rub-ber on the Geor-gia as-phalt, we got a lit-tle cra-zy but we

Fiddle Solo:
w/Rhy. Figs. 2 *(Gtr. 1)* **& 2A** *(Gtr. 2)*   **w/Fill 1**   *D.S. %% al Coda*

nev-er got ___ caught.

Coda

rit.

lit-tle 'bout love,   a lot a-bout liv-in' and a lit-tle 'bout ___ love.

That's right!

P.M.

Verses 2 & 4:
Well, we fogged up the windows in my old Chevy.
I was willin' but she wasn't ready.
So, I settled for a burger and a grape sno-cone.
I dropped her off early but I didn't go home.
(To Chorus:)

DEVIL WOMAN

Words and Music by
MARTY ROBBINS

*Gtr. 2 ad lib. on repeats a la Verse and Chorus.

Devil Woman – 3 – 2

40

Verse 2:
Mary is waiting and weeping,
Down in our shack by the sea.
Even after I've hurt her,
Mary's still in love with me.
Devil woman, it's over.
Trapped no more by your charms.
'Cause I don't wanna stay, I wanna get away,
Woman let go of my arm.
(To Chorus:)

Verse 3:
Devil woman, you're evil.
Like the dark coral reef.
Like the winds that bring high times,
You bring sorrow and grief.
Made me ashamed to face Mary,
Barely had the strength to tell.
Skies are not so black,
Mary took me back.
Mary has broken your spell.
(To Chorus:)

Verse 4:
Running along by the seashore,
Running as fast as I can.
Even the seagulls are happy,
Glad I'm coming home again.
Never again will I ever
Cause another tear to fall.
Down the beach I see what belongs to me,
The one I want most of all.
(To Chorus:)

Devil Woman – 3 – 3

GO REST HIGH ON THAT MOUNTAIN

Words and Music by
VINCE GILL

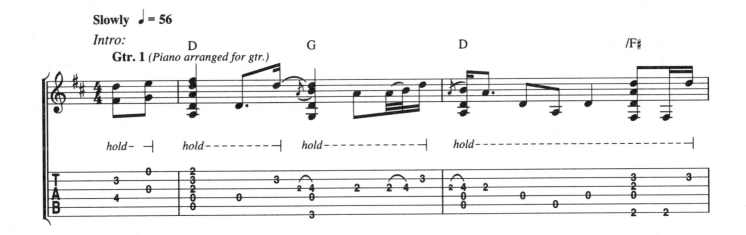

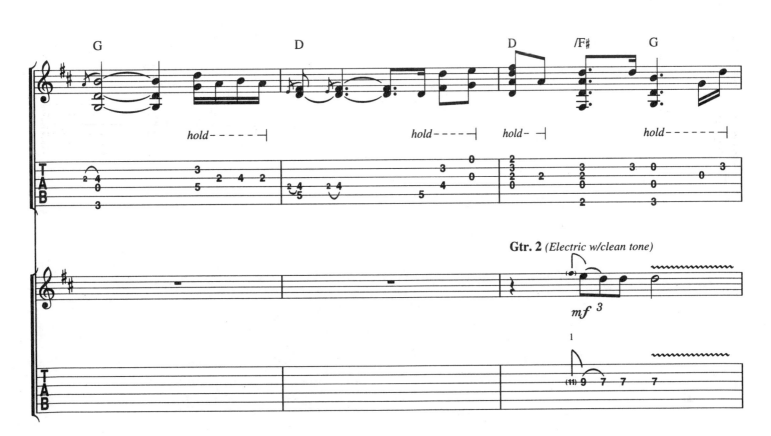

Go Rest High on that Mountain - 9 - 1

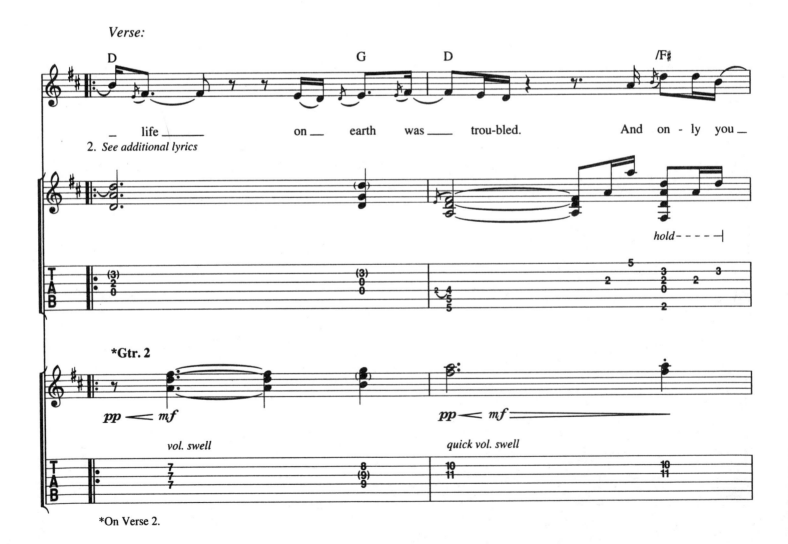

*On Verse 2.

*6th string = D; multiple gtrs. arranged for one gtr.

Verse 2:
Oh, how we cried the day you left us.
We gathered 'round your grave to grieve.
Wish I could see the angels' faces
When they hear your sweet voice sing.
So, go rest . . .
(To Chorus:)

DON'T IT MAKE MY BROWN EYES BLUE

Words and Music by
RICHARD LEIGH

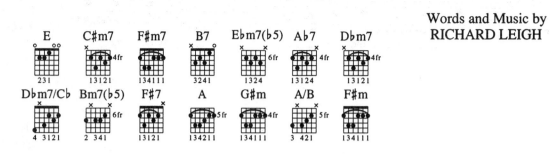

1. Don't know when
2. *See additional lyrics.*

I've been so ___ blue.

Don't know what's come o-ver you. ___ You've found some - one ___

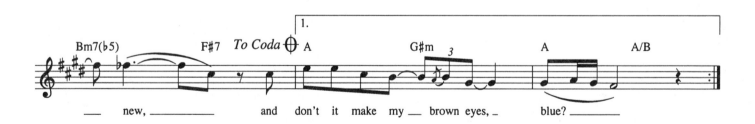

___ new, ___ and don't it make my ___ brown eyes, ___ blue? ___

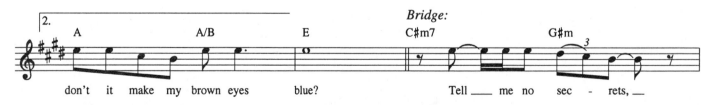

don't it make my brown eyes blue? Tell ___ me no sec - rets, ___

tell ___ me some lies. _____ Give me no ___ rea - sons, ___ give me ___

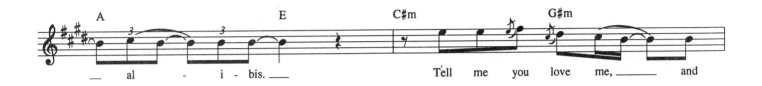

___ al - i - bis. _____ Tell me you love me, _____ and

D.S. 𝄋 al Coda

don't let me cry. ___ Say an - y - thing, _ but don't say good - bye. _____

Coda
Outro:

don't it make my brown eyes, don't it make my brown eyes, don't it make my brown eyes

Outro:
Repeat & fade

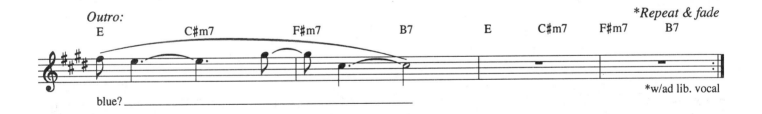

blue? _____

*w/ad lib. vocal

Verse 2:
I'll be fine when you're gone,
I'll just cry all night long.
Say it isn't true.
(To Bridge:)

Verse 3:
I didn't mean to treat you bad,
Didn't know just what I had.
But honey, now I do. And . . . .
(To Coda)

Don't it Make My Brown Eyes Blue – 2 – 2

DON'T ROCK THE JUKEBOX

Words and Music by
ALAN JACKSON, KEITH STEGALL
and ROGER MURRAH

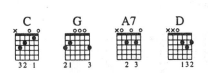

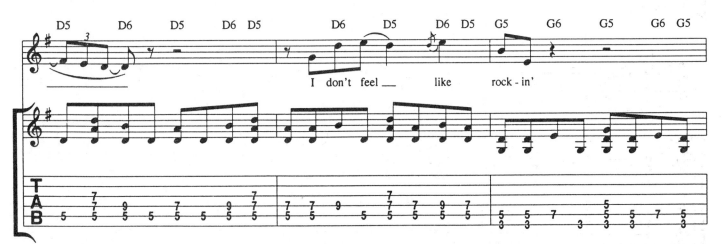

Don't Rock the Jukebox – 6 – 1

54

standin' here in line.___ I've been down ___ and lone-
(Cont. in slashes)

Gtr. 2

-ly ___ ev-er since she left.___ Be-fore you punch that

num-ber, ___ could I make ___ one re - quest? ___ Don't rock the juke-

Chorus:
G5   G6 G5   G6   C5   C6 C5   C6   C5   C6 C5   C6

-box,   I wan-na hear   some Jones. _____

Don't Rock the Jukebox – 6 – 4

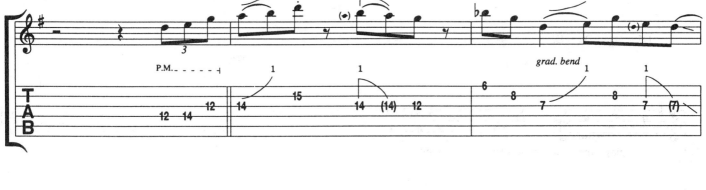

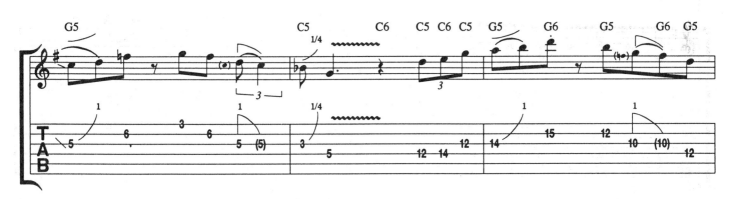

Verse 2:

Now I ain't got nothin' against rock and roll
But when your heart's been broken, you need a song that's slow.
There ain't nothin' like a steel guitar to drown a memory.
Before you spend your money, baby, play a song for me.

(To Chorus:)

Don't Rock the Jukebox – 6 – 6

DON'T TAKE THE GIRL

Words and Music by
CRAIG MARTIN and LARRY W. JOHNSON

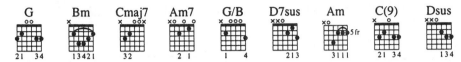

Slowly ♩ = 52

Intro:
Gtr. 2

Verse:
Gtr. 1 *Cont. fingerpicking simile*

1. John-ny's dad-dy was tak-ing him fish - in' ___ when he was eight years old. ___
2. 3. *See additional lyrics.*

A lit - tle girl ___ came through ___ the ___ front ___ gate ___ hold-in' a fish-in' pole. ___

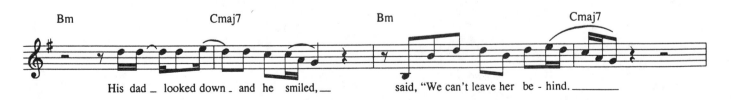

His dad ___ looked down ___ and he smiled, ___ said, "We can't leave her be - hind. ___

Don't Take the Girl – 2 – 1

Son, I know you don't want her to go, but some-day you'll change your mind." And John - ny said,

"Take Jim-my John-son, take Tom-my Thomp - son, take my best - friend, Bo.

Take an - y - bod - y that you want as long as she don't go. Take an - y boy in the world,

Dad - dy please, don't take the girl.

1. 2.

w/ Rhy. Fig. 1 *(Gtr.2, 2 meas. only, last time)*

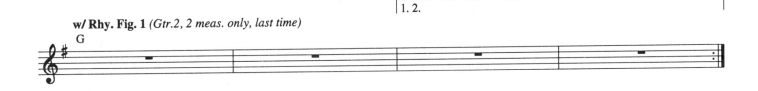

3.

John - ny's dad - dy was tak - ing him fish - ing when he was eight years old.

Verse 2:
Same ol' boy, same sweet girl, ten years down the road.
He held her tight and kissed her lips in front of the picture show.
A stranger came and pulled a gun and grabbed her by the arm.
Said, "If you do what I tell you to, there won't be any harm."
And Johnny said,
"Take my money, take my wallet, take my credit cards.
Here's the watch that my grandpa gave me, here's the keys to my car.
Mr., give it a whirl, but please, don't take the girl."

Verse 3:
Same ol' boy, same sweet girl, five years down the road.
There's gonna be a little one and she says, "It's time to go."
Doctor said, "The baby's fine but, you'll have to leave
'Cause his mama's fadin' fast," and Johnny hit his knees.
And then he prayed,
"Take the very breath you gave me, take the heart from my chest.
I'll gladly take her place if you'll have me.
Make this my last request.
Take me out of this world, God, please, don't take the girl."

Don't Take The Girl – 2 – 2

EL PASO

Words and Music by
MARTY ROBBINS

El Paso – 4 – 1

62

El Paso – 4 – 3

Verse 3:
So in anger, I challenged his right
For the love of this maiden.
Down went his hand for the gun that he wore.

Verse 4:
My challenge was answered in less than a heartbeat.
The handsome young stranger lay dead on the floor.
Just for a moment, I stood there in silence,
Shocked by the foul, evil deed I had done.
Many thoughts raced through my mind as I stood there,
I had but one chance, and that was to run.

Chorus 2:
Out through the back door of Rosa's I ran.
Out where the horses were tied.
I caught a good one, it looked like it could run.
Up on its back, and away I did ride just as fast as I...

Verse 5:
Could from the west Texas town of El Paso,
Out to the badlands of New Mexico.
Back in El Paso my life would be worthless.
Everything's gone in life, nothing is left.
It's been so long since I've seen the young maiden.
My love is stronger than my fear of death.

Chorus 3:
I saddled up and away I did go,
Riding alone in the dark.
Maybe tomorrow a bullet may find me,
Tonight nothing's worse than the pain in my heart.
And at last, here I...

Verse 6:
Am on the hill, overlooking El Paso.
I can see Rosa's Cantina below.
My love is strong and it pushes me onward,
Down off the hill to Felina I go.
Off to my right, I see five mounted cowboys,
Off to my left ride a dozen and more.
Shouting and shooting, I can't let them catch me,
I have to make it to Rosa's back door.
(To Chorus 4:)

Chorus 4:
Something is dreadfully wrong, for I feel
A deep burning pain in my side.
Though I am trying to stay in the saddle,
I'm getting weary, unable to ride.
But my love for...
(To Verse 7:)

Verse 7:
Felina is strong and I rise where I've fallen,
Though I am weary, I can't stop to rest.
I see the white puff of smoke from the rifle,
I feel the bullet go deep in my chest.
From out of nowhere, Felina has found me,
Kissing my cheek as she kneels by my side.
Cradled by two loving arms that I'll die for,
One farewell kiss and Felina goodbye.

El Paso – 4 – 4

FOREVER'S AS FAR AS I'LL GO

Words and Music by
MIKE REID

Verse 2:

When there's age around my eyes and grey in your hair,
And it only takes a touch to recall the love we've shared.
I won't take for granted that you know my love is true.
Each night in your arms, I will whisper to you...

(To Chorus:)

I CROSS MY HEART

Words and Music by
STEVE DORFF and
ERIC KAZ

I Cross My Heart – 4 – 1

I Cross My Heart – 4 - 2

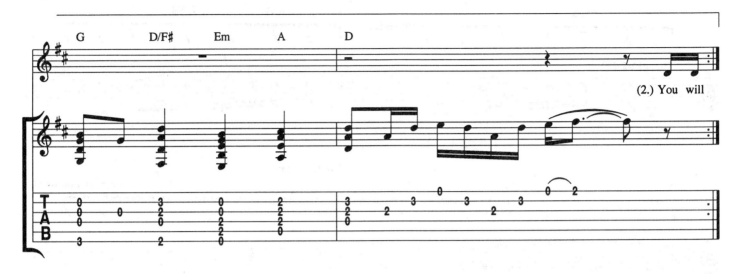

(2.) You will

Bridge:

mine. ___

And if a-long the way ___ we find the day ___

it starts ___ to storm, ___ you've got the prom-ise of ___ my love ___ to

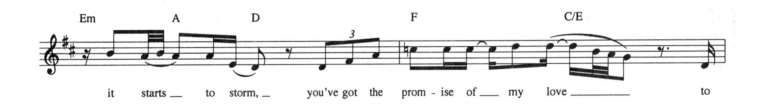

Instrumental Solo:

keep ___ you ___ warm. ___

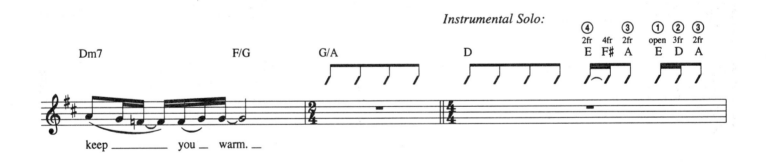

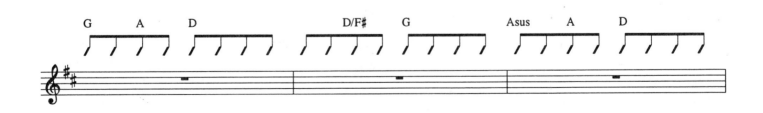

Verse 2:

You will always be the miracle
That makes my life complete.
And as long as there's a breath in me,
I'll make yours just as sweet.
As we look into the future,
It's as far as we can see.
So let's make each tomorrow
Be the best that it can be.

(To Chorus:)

GONE COUNTRY

By
BOB McDILL

Gone Country – 5 – 1

72

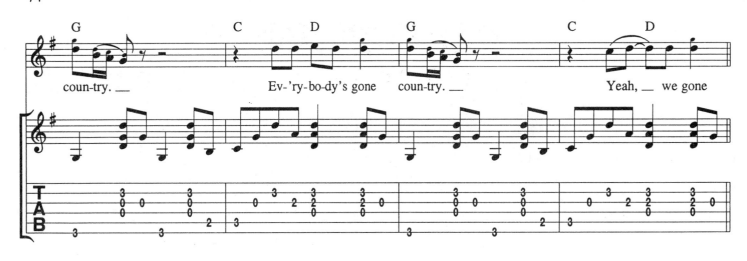

coun-try. ___   Ev-'ry-bo-dy's gone   coun-try. ___   Yeah, ___ we gone

Outro: *Repeat & fade*

coun-try. ___   The whole   world's ‿ gone   coun-try. ___
                                                             gone ‿ coun-try. ___

Vocals tacet after 1st time.

Verse 2:

Well, the folk scene's dead,
But he's holding out in the village.
He's been writing songs,
Speaking out against wealth and privilege.
He says, "I don't believe in money,
But a man could make himself a killin'.
'Cause some of that stuff
Don't sound much different from Dylan.
I hear down there it's changed, you see.
They're not as backward as they used to be."

Chorus 2 & 3:

He's gone country, look as them boots.
He's gone country, back to his roots.
He's gone country, a new kind of suit.
He's gone country, here he comes.

Verse 3:

He commutes to L.A.,
But he's got a house in the valley.
But the bills are piling up
And the pop scene just ain't on a rally.
He says, "Honey, I'm a serious composer,
Schooled in voice and composition.
But with the crime and the smog these days,
This ain't no place for children.
Lord, it sounds so easy, this shouldn't take long.
Be back in the money in no time at all."

Chorus 4:

Yeah, he's gone country, a new kind of walk.
He's gone country, a new kind of talk.
He's gone country, look at them boots.
He's gone country, oh, back to his roots.
(To Coda)

HALF THE MAN

By CLINT BLACK
and HAYDEN NICHOLAS

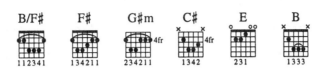

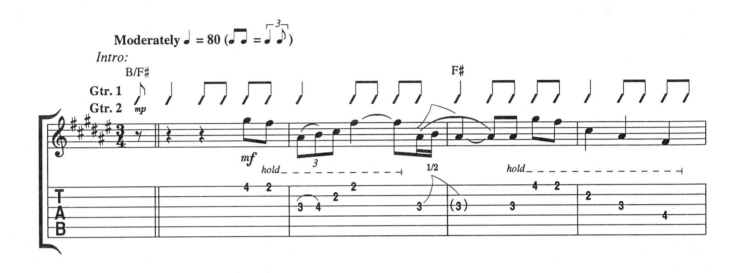

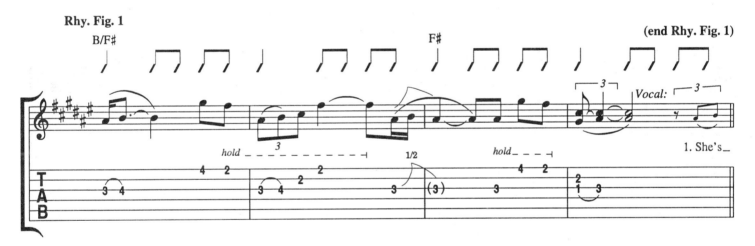

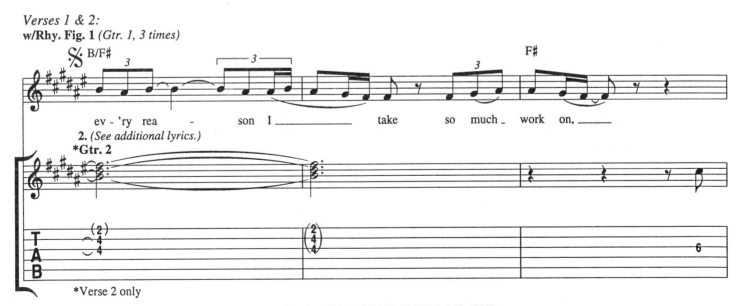

*Verse 2 only

Half The Man – 5 – 1

Verse 2:

When the rivers all run dry, she finds the water.
And when everything is dark, she finds the light.
And when its time to fly, she's flying with me.
With her on the wing, we balance out just right.

(To Chorus:)

I LOVE THE WAY YOU LOVE ME

Capo 1st fret

Slowly ♩ = 72

Intro:

Words and Music by
VICTORIA SHAW and
CHUCK CANNON

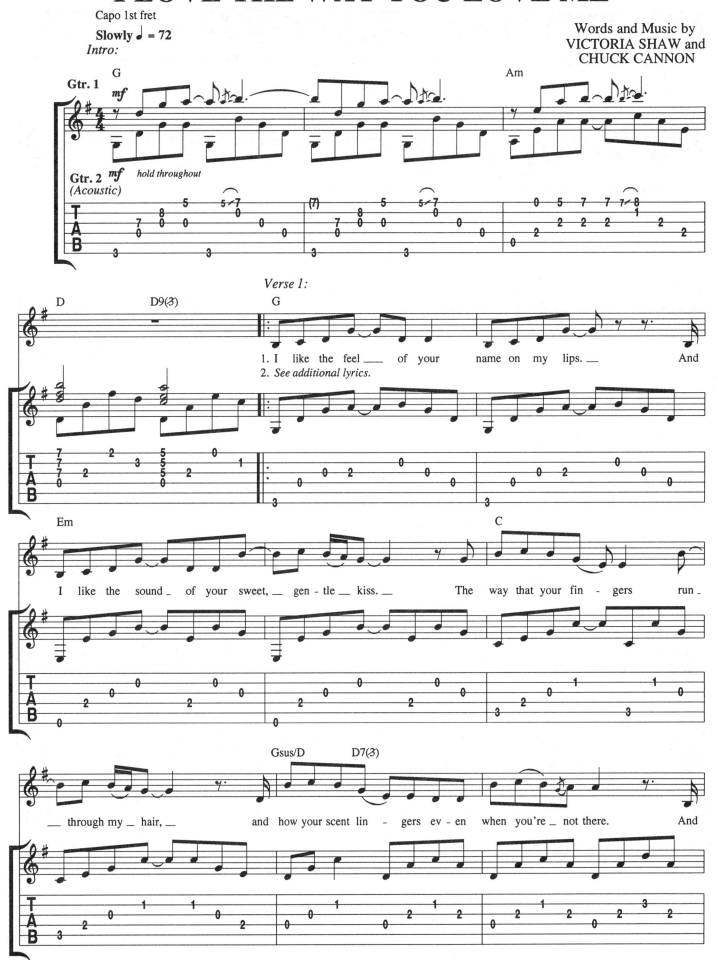

Verse 1:

1. I like the feel ___ of your name on my lips. ___ And
2. *See additional lyrics.*

I like the sound ___ of your sweet, ___ gen-tle ___ kiss. ___ The way that your fin-gers run ___

___ through my ___ hair, ___ and how your scent lin - gers ev - en when you're ___ not there. And

I Love The Way You Love Me - 4 - 1

I Love The Way You Love Me – 4 – 2

Strong_ and wild,_____ slow_ and ea - sy,___ heart_ and soul_ so_ com - plete - ly, I____ love_____ the way_____ you love_ __ me._____

Bridge:

And I could list___ a mil - lion things_____

Verse 2:

I like to imitate ol' Jerry Lee
While you roll your eyes when I'm slightly off key.
And I like the innocent way that you cry
At sappy old movies you've seen hundreds of times.

(To Chorus:)

I Love The Way You Love Me – 4 – 4

I STILL BELIEVE IN YOU

Words and Music by
VINCE GILL and JOHN BARLOW JARVIS

I Still Believe in You – 3 – 2

Verse 2:
Somewhere along the way I guess I just lost track,
Only thinkin' of myself, and never lookin' back.
For all the times I've hurt you, I apologize,
I'm sorry it took so long to finally realize.
Give me the chance to prove that nothing's worth losing you.
(To Chorus:)

I DON'T EVEN KNOW YOUR NAME

Words and Music by
ALAN JACKSON, RON JACKSON
and ANDY LOFTIN

*Acoustic gtr.

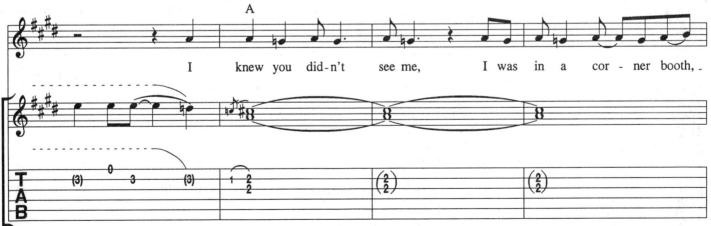

Guitar Solo:

Gtr. 1 *Cont. rhy. simile*

Gtr. 3

Gtr. 2

w/**Rhy. Fill 1** *(Gtr. 1) simile*

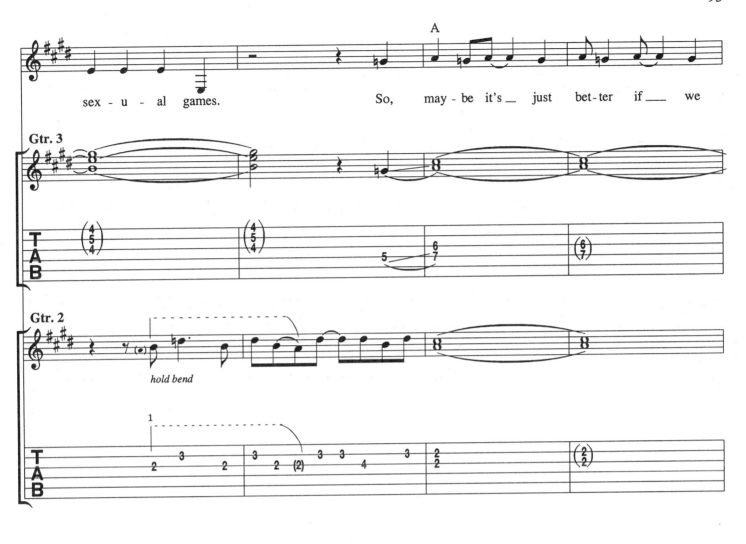

Half time feel

ev - en know __ her name.

Get me out - ta here!

Fiddle Solo:
Gtr. 1 *Cont. rhy. simile*
Gtr. 2

w/Rhy. Fill 1 *(Gtr. 1)*

w/Riff A *(Gtr. 1)*

Pedal Steel Solo 2:
Gtrs. 1 & 2 *Cont. rhy. simile*

Gtr. 3

Acoustic Gtr. Solo:
Gtrs. 1 & 2 *Cont. rhy. simile*

w/Rhy. Fill 1 *(Gtr. 1)*

w/Rhy. Fig. 1 *(Gtr. 1)*
simile

Electric Gtr. Solo 2:

I Don't Even Know Your Name – 15 – 14

Verse 2:
So, I ordered straight tequilla, a little courage in a shot.
I asked you for a date and then I asked to tie the knot.
I got a little wasted, yeah, I went a little far.
But I finally got to hug you when you helped me to my car.
The last thing I remember I heard myself say:
I'm in love with you, baby, and I don't even know your name.
(To Chorus:)

IF THERE HADN'T BEEN YOU

Words and Music by
TOM SHAPIRO and RON SHELLARD

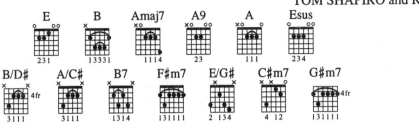

If There Hadn't Been You – 4 – 1

104

Verse 2:

A man, filled with hope
Who finally knows where he belongs.
A heart, filled with love,
More than enough to keep it strong.
A life that's alive again,
No longer afraid to face the truth.
All of this I would have missed
If there hadn't been you.

(To Chorus:)

If There Hadn't Been You – 4 – 4

IF TOMORROW NEVER COMES

Words and Music by
KENT BLAZY and GARTH BROOKS

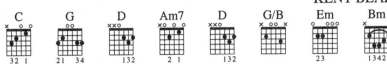

Chorus:

Verse 2:
'Cause I've lost loved ones in my life,
Who never knew how much I loved them.
Now I live with the regret that my
True feelings for them never were revealed.
So I made a promise to myself to say
Each day how much she means to me.
And avoid that circumstance where there's no
Second chance to tell her how I feel.
(To Chorus:)

If Tomorrow Never Comes – 4 – 4

ON THE ROAD AGAIN

Words and Music by
WILLIE NELSON

On The Road Again - 4 - 2

112

On The Road Again - 4 - 4

CRYING

Words and Music by
ROY ORBISON and
JOE MELSON

Crying - 2 - 1

Verse 2:
I thought that I was over you,
But it's true, so true.
I love you even more than I did before,
But darling, what I can I do?
For you don't love me, and I'll always be...

Chorus 2:
Crying over you,
Crying over you.
Yes, now you're gone and from this moment on
I'll be crying, crying, crying, crying.
Yeah, crying, crying over you.

UNCLOUDY DAY

TRADITIONAL
Arrangement by WILLIE NELSON

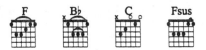

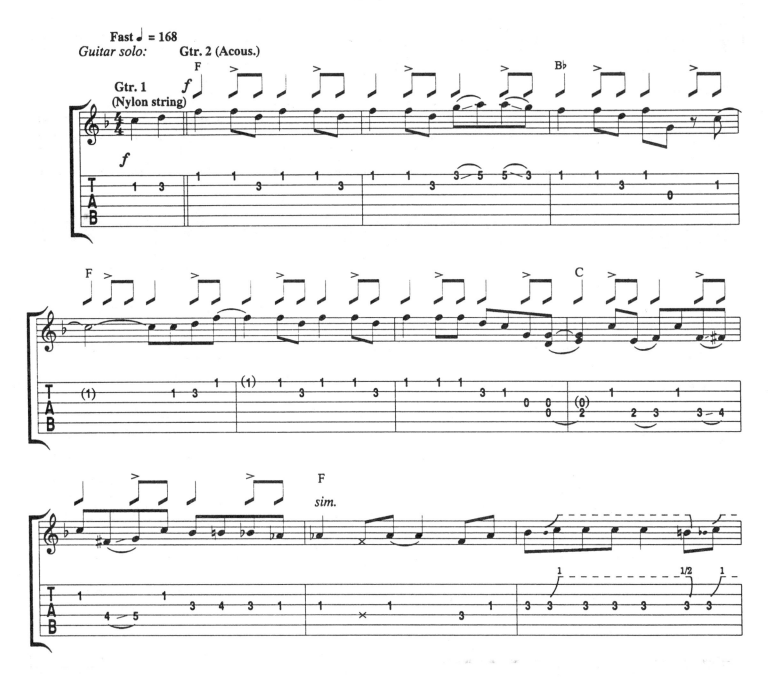

Uncloudy Day - 2 - 1

Verses 1, 2, & 3:

me of a home far beyond the skies. And they tell me of a home far away.

2. 3. *See additional lyrics.*

far a-way. Oh they tell me of a home where no storm clouds rise,

Chorus:

oh they tell me of an un-cloud-y day. Oh, the land of

cloud-less days, oh, the land of an un-cloud-ed sky. Oh they tell me of a home

4th time to Coda

where no storm-clouds rise, oh they tell me of an un-cloud-y day.

Solos: Piano (1st time) slide gtr. (2nd time)
organ (3rd time)
Rhy. Gtr. play verse form 1 time for each solo
17

Coda

day.

Verse 2:
Well they tell me of a home where my friends have gone.
And they tell me of that land far away.
Where the dream of life and eternal bloom
shares its fragrance through the uncloudy day.

Verse 3:
Oh they tell me of the King and his beauty there,
And they tell me that mine eyes shall behold
where he sits on the throne that is whiter
than snow in the city that is made of gold.

Verse 4:
Oh they tell me that he smiles on his children there.
And his smile drives their sorrows away.
And they tell me that no tears will ever come again,
in that lovely land of uncloudy days.

I WILL ALWAYS LOVE YOU

Words and Music by
DOLLY PARTON

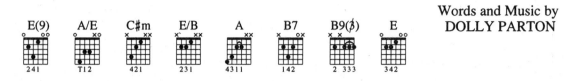

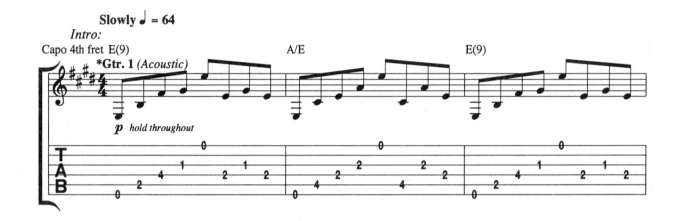

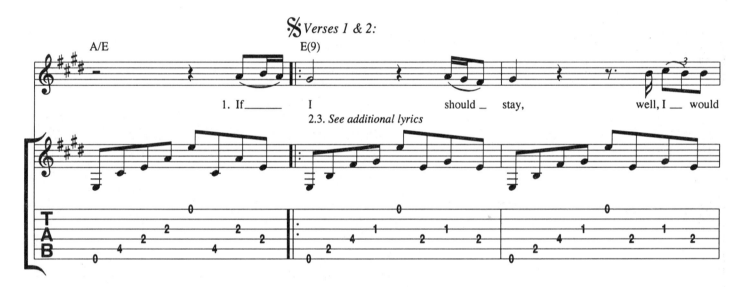

I Will Always Love You – 3 – 2

*Played by bass gtr.

IN THIS LIFE

Words and Music by
MIKE REID and
ALLEN SHAMBLIN

only dream that mattered had come true. In this life, I was loved by you. In this life, I was loved by you.

Outro:
C (Gtr. 1 play intro figure)
you.

Gtr. 2 *(Nylon string acoustic)*

Verse 2:
For every mountain I have climbed,
Every raging river crossed,

You were the treasure that I longed to find,
Without your love, I would be lost.
(To Chorus:)

In This Life – 3 – 3

JESUS AND MAMA

Words and Music by
DANNY BEAR MAYO and
JAMES DEAN HICKS

126

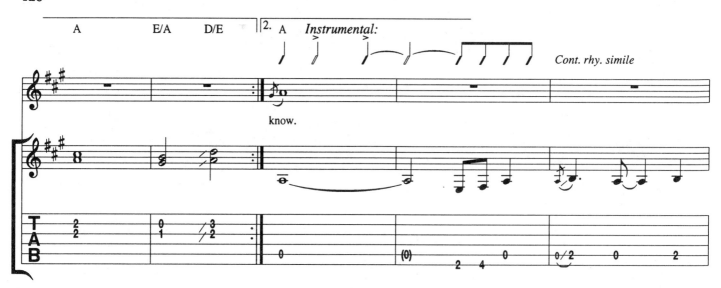

know.

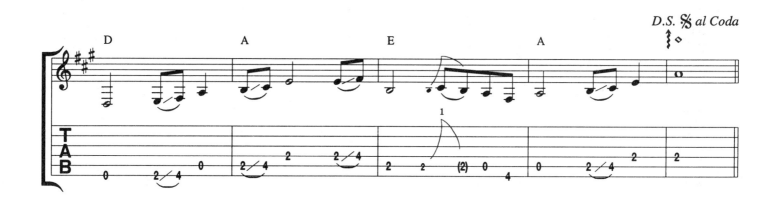

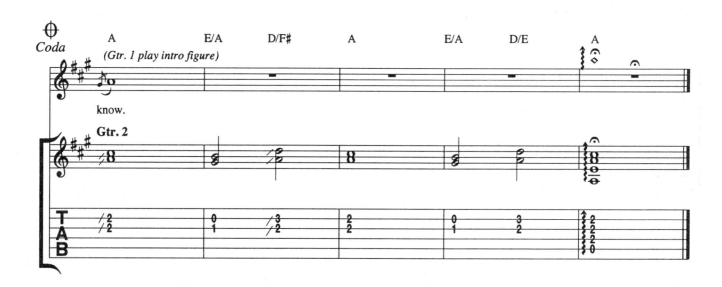

Coda

know.

Verse 2:

I felt trapped most all of my life,
Found new kinds of lows and highs.
Never been a husband, but I've had a lot of wives hold me.
Headstrong, stubborn, couldn't be told.
Like a wild horse that couldn't be rode.
A rainbow chaser hungry for gold,
And still searchin'.

(To Chorus:)

Verse 3:

I wish mom could see me now,
And how I've turned it all around.
Lately, I've been goin' down the right road.
Life's a picture that you paint
With blues and grays, cans and can'ts.
Heaven knows I'm not a saint, but I know...

(To Chorus:)

POINT OF LIGHT

Words and Music by
DON SCHLITZ and
TOM SCHUYLER

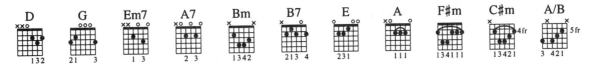

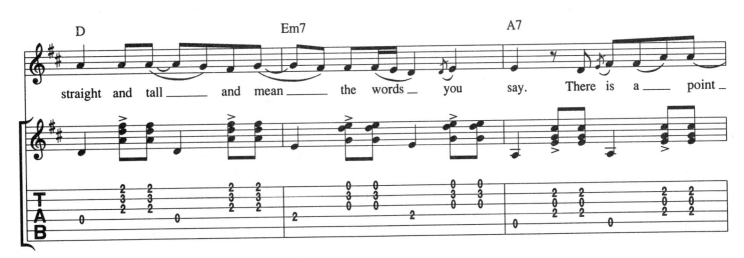

you must __ de - cide _____ just to do it 'cause ____ it's right; __

__ ____ that's when you _____ be - come _____ a point ____ of _____

__ light. ____ There is a ____ dark - ness __ that ev -

- 'ry - one _____ must face. __ It wants to take _____ what's

good and fair _____ and lay ____ it all ____ to waste. __ And that dark -

- ness _____ ____ cov - ers ev - 'ry - thing __ in

sight, _ un - til it meets _____ a sin - gle point _ of _____

light. All it takes is a

point of light. A ray of hope

in the dark - est night. If you

see what's wrong and you try to make it

right, you will be a

Chorus:

D.S. 𝄋 al Coda

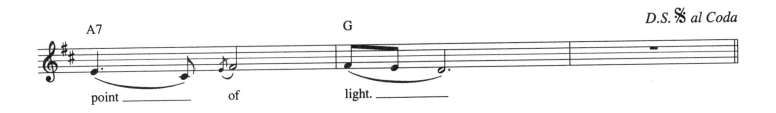

point of light.

Coda

Verse 3:

There are dream - ers who are mak -

-ing dreams ___ come true, ___ tak-ing time ___ to teach ___ the chil-

-dren ___ there's noth-ing they ___ can't ___ do. ___ Giv-ing

shel - ter to ___ the home - less, giv-ing hope ___ to those ___ with - out. ___

___ Is - n't that ___ what this ___ land's all ___ a - bout? __

Bridge:

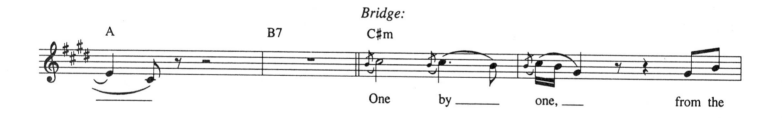

___ One by _____ one, ___ from the

moun - tains to ___ the sea, ___ points ___ of light ___

___ are call-ing out ___ to you ___ and me. _____

Chorus:

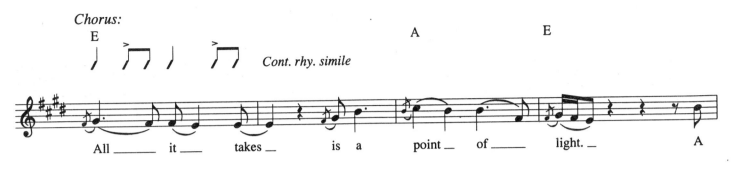

All _____ it _____ takes _____ is a point _____ of _____ light. _____

ray _____ of _____ hope in the dark - est _____ night. If you

see _____ what's _ wrong _ and you try to make _____ it _____ right, _____

you _____ will be _____ a point _____ of light. _____

1. 2. If you

Verse 2:
There are heroes whose names we never hear,
A dedicated army of quiet volunteers.
Reaching out to feed the hungry,
Reaching out to save the land,
Reaching out to help their fellow man.
(To Verse 3:)

LIVIN' ON LOVE

Words and Music by
ALAN JACKSON

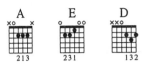

Verse 3:
Two old people without a thing.
Children gone, but still they sing side by side
In that front porch swing, livin' on love.
He can't see anymore,
She can barely sweep the floor.
Hand in hand they'll walk through that door,
Just livin' on love.
(To Chorus:)

LIZA JANE

Words and Music by
VINCE GILL and REED NIELSEN

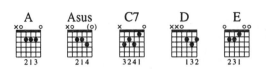

*Use left hand thumb.

w/Rhy. Fig. 2 *(Gtrs. 1 & 3) simile*

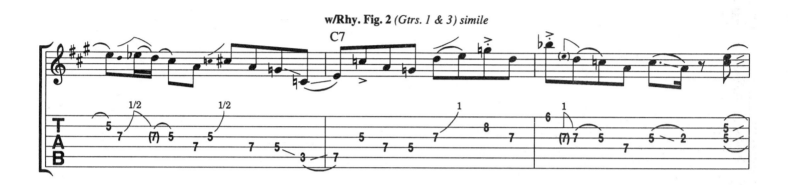

w/Rhy. Fig. 1 *(Gtrs. 1, 2 & 3) simile*

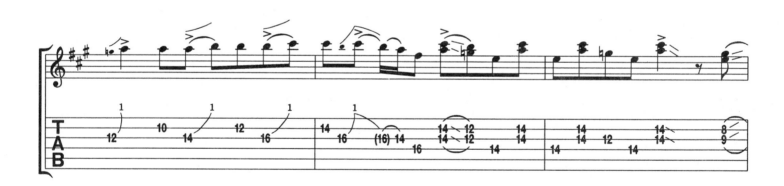

w/Rhy. Fig. 2 *(Gtrs. 1 & 3) simile*

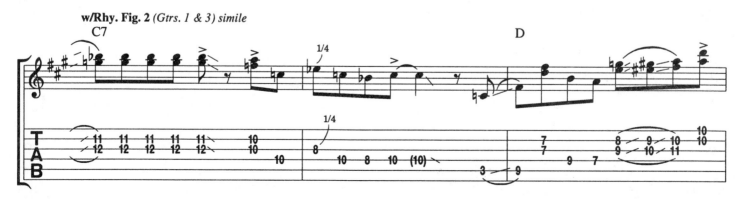

Verse 2:
You got that body, you got that frame.
So why don't you call me little Liza Jane?
(To Chorus:)

Verse 3:
Now, you've heard my story,
You got to know my name.
So why don't you call me little Liza Jane?
(To Chorus:)

Liza Jane – 6 – 6

GOOD HEARTED WOMAN

Words and Music by
WAYLON JENNINGS and
WILLIE NELSON

Fast country double time ♩ = 144

Intro:

Gtr.1 (Nylon string)

* Hold notes to form chords at your discretion

Verses 1 and 2:

1. Well, a-long___ time for-got-ten,   her dreams___
2. *See additional lyrics.*

hold ----------------------

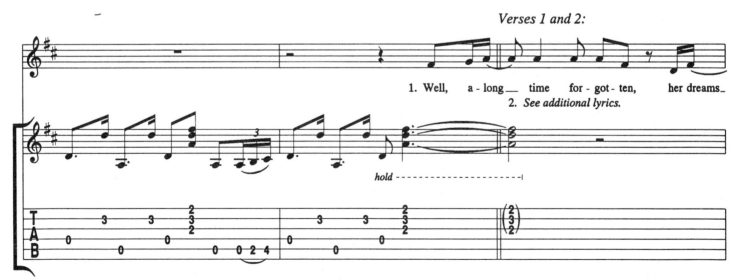

Good Hearted Woman - 6 - 1

Chorus:

and all the good times to come.   She's a

good-heart-ed wo-man in love with a good-tim-in' man.

And she loves him in spite of his ways that she don't_ un-der-stand.

Through tear-drops and laugh-ter_ they're gon-na'

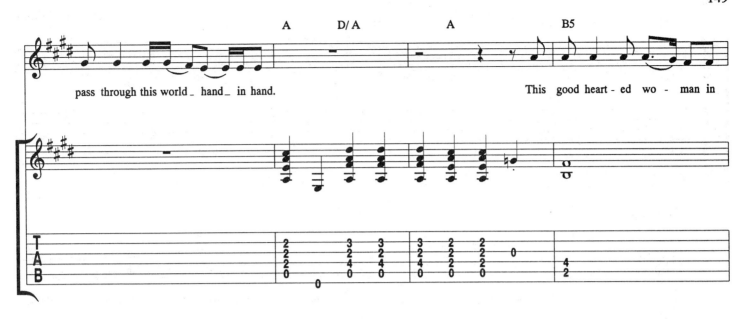

pass through this world hand in hand.   This good heart-ed wo-man in

love with a good-tim - in' man.

Verse 2:

He likes the night life;
　　the bright lights and his good timin' friends.
And when the party's all over
　　she'll welcome him back home again.
Y'all know she don't understand him,
　　she does the best that she can.
She's a good hearted woman
　　in love with a good timin' man.

LOVE, ME

Words and Music by
SKIP EWING and MAX T. BARNES

Slowly ♩ = 54

1. I read a note _ my grand-ma wrote back in __ nine-teen __ twen-ty *three.* __
2. 3. *See aditional lyrics.*

Grand-pa kept __ it in __ his coat and he showed it once _ to __ me. __ He said,

Love, Me – 4 – 1

Love, Me – 4 – 2

tween now and then ___ 'til I see you a gain, ___ I'll be lov-ing ___ you, ___ love, me." ___

Verse 2:

We had this crazy plan to meet
And run away together;
Get married in the first town we came to
And live forever.
But nailed to the tree where we were
Supposed to meet,
Instead I found this letter,
And this is what it said.

(To Chorus:)

Verse 3:

I read those words just hours before
My grandma passed away,
In the doorway of a church where me and
Grandpa stopped to pray.
I know I'd never seen him cry
In all my fifteen years,
But as he said these words to her,
His eyes filled up with tears.

(To Chorus:)

THE MOST BEAUTIFUL GIRL

Words and Music by
NORRIS WILSON, BILLY SHERRILL
and RORY BOURKE

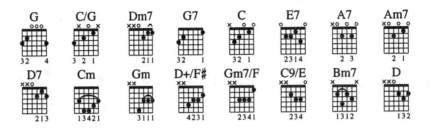

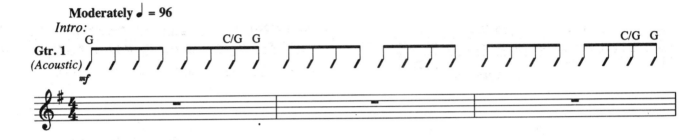

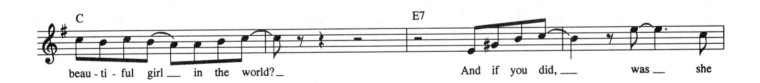

The Most Beautiful Girl - 2 - 1

The Most Beautiful Girl – 2 – 2

NEVER KNEW LONELY

Words and Music by
VINCE GILL

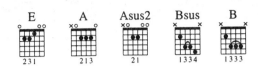

*Two gtrs. arranged for one gtr.

ba - by, __ I'm ____ scared. __ I nev - er knew __ lone - ly __ 'til __

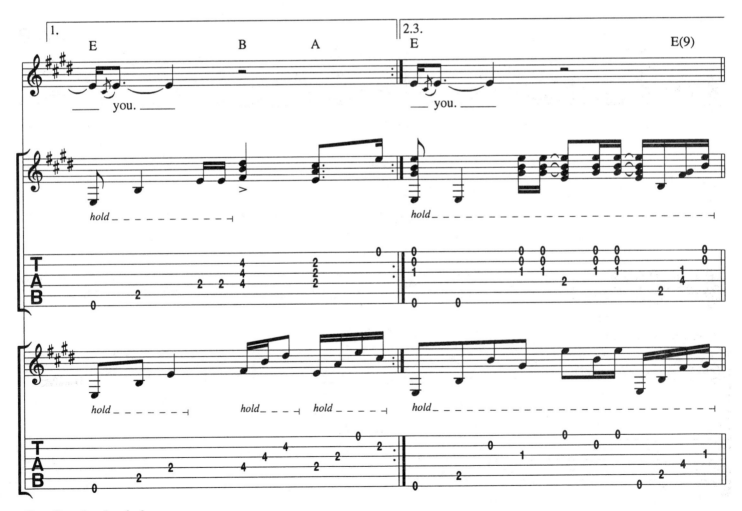

___ you. ___ ___ you. ___

Chorus:

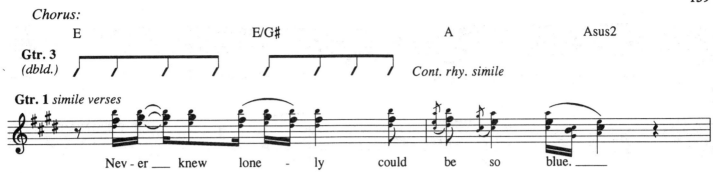

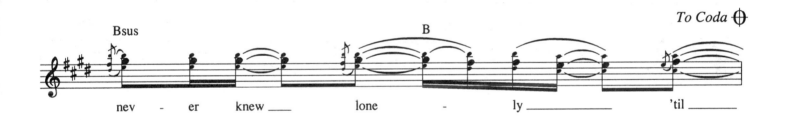

Guitar Solo:

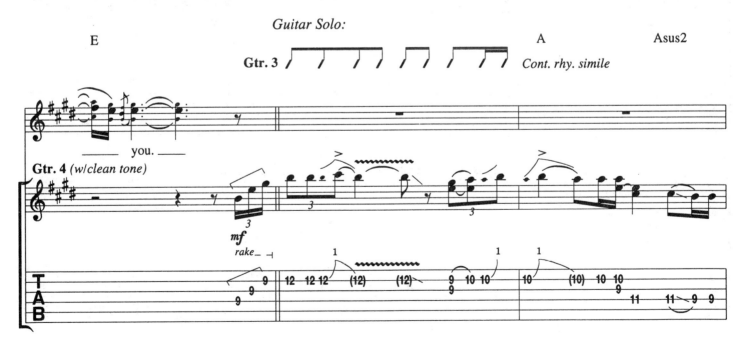

Never Knew Lonely – 6 – 4

Verse 2:
You are my rock and the strength I need
To keep me sane in this life that I lead.
Now, I'm not with you and my broken heart beats,
I never knew lonely 'til you.
(To Chorus:)

Verse 3:
And I can't make up for the times I've been gone.
I'll prove I love you in the words of this song.
Back in your arms, girl, it's where I belong.
I never knew lonely 'til you.
(To Chorus:)

FAST AS YOU

Words and Music by
DWIGHT YOAKAM

*Double tracked throughout.

1. May-be some-day I'll__ be strong._____ May-be it__ won't__ be long.__
2. See additional lyrics

Fast As You - 9 - 1

Fast As You - 9 - 2

I'll be the one— who's strong.

You'll be the one who's gon-na cry.

You're gon-na cry like me.—

We'll just, uh, wait and see.

Fast As You - 9 - 7

Fast As You - 9 - 8

Verse 2:
Maybe I'll do things right.
Maybe I'll start tonight.
You'll learn to cry like me.
Baby, let's just wait and see.
Maybe I'll start tonight
And do things right.

PAPA LOVED MAMA

Words and Music by
KIM WILLIAMS and GARTH BROOKS

Gtr. 2 tuned:
⑥= E ③= G
⑤= A ②= B
④= D ①= D

Fast ♩ = 160

Intro:
Gtr. 1
(Acoustic)
N.C.(E7)
Riff A

w/Riff A (1st 3 bars only)
Gtr. 2
(end Riff A)

Verse:

1. Pa - pa drove a truck near-ly all his life; you know it drove Ma-ma cra-zy be-ing a
2. See additional lyrics.

*Gtr. 1 cont. in slashes

(Cont. rhy. simile)

truck-er's wife.   The part she could-n't han-dle was the be-ing a - lone,__ I guess she

Papa Loved Mama – 5 – 1

Papa Loved Mama –5 – 3

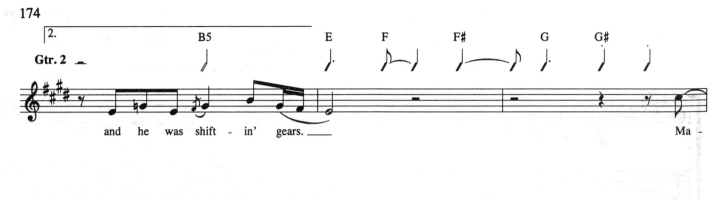

and he was shift - in' gears. ___ Ma-

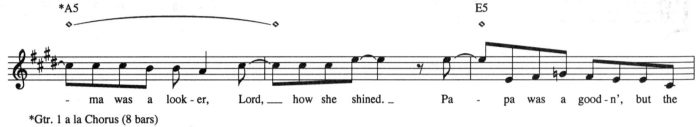

- ma was a look - er, Lord, ___ how she shined. __ Pa - pa was a good-n', but the

*Gtr. 1 a la Chorus (8 bars)

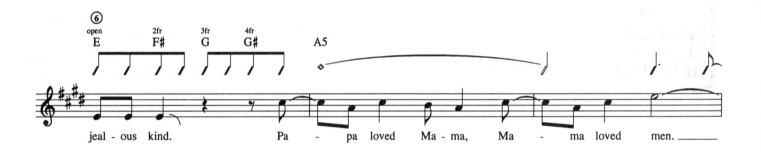

jeal - ous kind. Pa - pa loved Ma - ma, Ma - ma loved men. ___

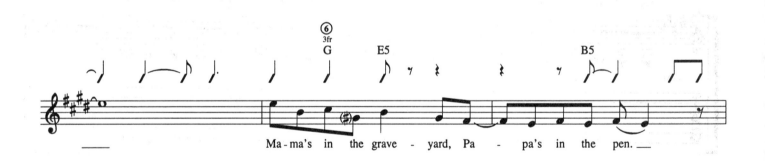

___ Ma - ma's in the grave - yard, Pa - pa's in the pen. __

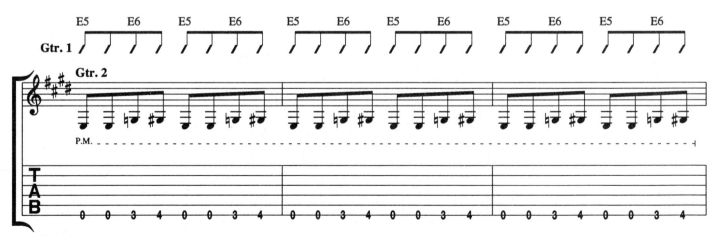

Papa Loved Mama – 5 – 4

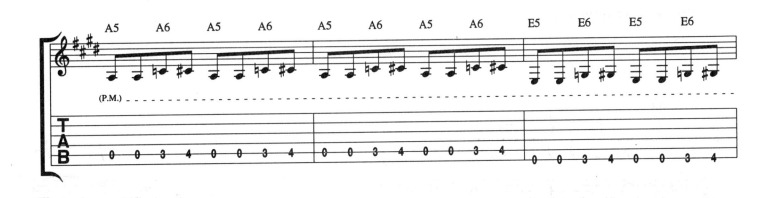

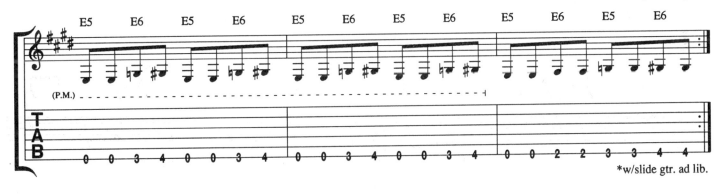

Verse 2:
Well, it was bound to happen and one night it did,
Papa came home and it was just us kids.
He had a dozen roses and a bottle of wine,
If he was lookin' to surprise us, he was doin' fine.
I heard him cry for Mama up and down the hall,
Then I heard a bottle break against the bedroom wall.
That old diesel engine made an eerie sound,
When papa fired it up and headed into town.

Chorus 2:
Well, the picture in the paper showed the scene real well,
Papa's rig was buried in the local motel.
The desk clerk said he saw it all real clear.
He never hit the brakes and he was shifting gears.
(To Chorus 1:)

PUT YOURSELF IN MY SHOES

Words and Music by
CLINT BLACK, HAYDEN NICHOLAS
and SHAKE RUSSELL

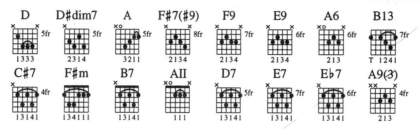

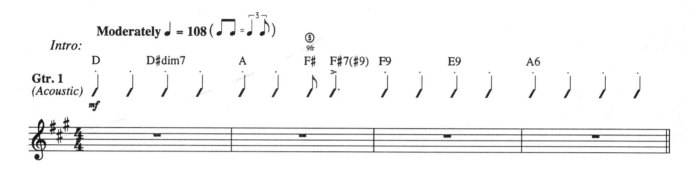

Intro:

Verse 1:

Gtr. 1, *Rhy. cont. simile*

1. Your mind is made up, you won't e - ven try, __ you did-n't e - ven cry __ this time. __
2. *See additional lyrics.*

You say that we can nev-er see eye _____ to eye, __ and one of us just must be blind. __

We have our dif-f'ren-ces, __ we're still ____ the same, __ see what we all __ want __ to see. __

Put Yourself in My Shoes – 3 – 1

Put Yourself in My Shoes – 3 – 2

Gtr. 2 tacet
Rhy. cont. simile

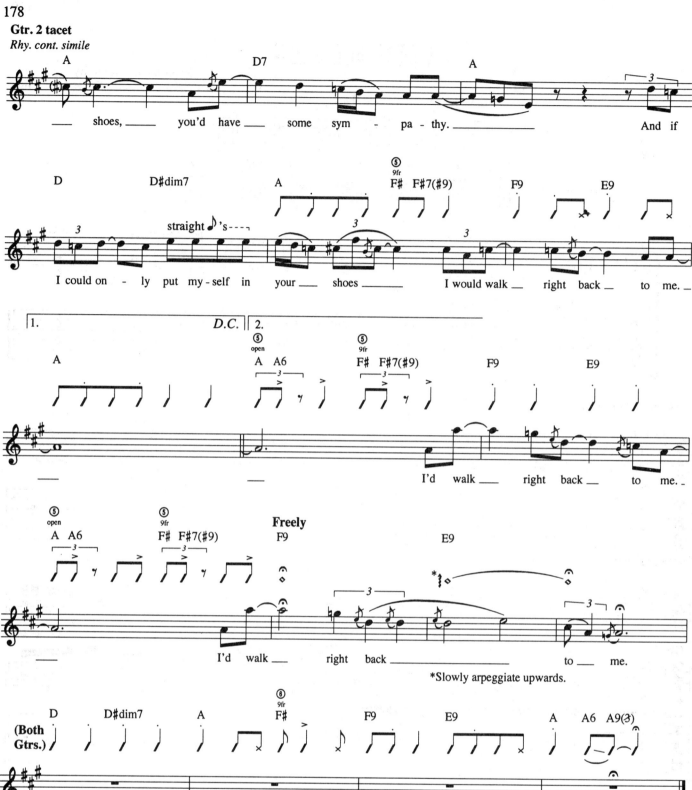

Verse 2:

You're gonna keep walkin' and
You're gonna pass me by.
You say you don't even care.
But I could always recognize a real goodbye,
And I know your heart's not there.
We've had our differences,
We're still the same,
Hear what we want to hear.
Now I'm head over heels in the lost and found.
It's a cryin' shame.
I thought we made the perfect pair.

(To Chorus:)

THE RIVER

**Words and Music by
VICTORIA SHAW and GARTH BROOKS**

*Chorus:

*Gtr. 1 continue fingerpicking a la Verses 1 & 2.

Verse 2:
Too many times we stand aside
And let the waters slip away
'Til what we put off 'til tomorrow
Has now become today.

So, don't you sit upon the shoreline
And say you're satisfied.
Choose to chance the rapids
And dare to dance the tide. Yes, I will. . .
(To Chorus:)

RODEO

Words and Music by
LARRY B. BASTIAN

*Repeat & fade

*w/ad lib. lead guitar

Verse 2:
She does her best to hold him
When his love comes to call.
But his need for it controls him
And her back's against the wall.
And it's, "So long, girl, I'll see you.",
When it's time for him to go.
You know the woman wants her cowboy
Like he wants his rodeo.
(To Chorus:)

Verse 3:
It'll drive a cowboy crazy.
It'll drive the man insane.
And he'll sell off everything he owns
Just to pay to play her game.
And a broken home and some broken bones
Is all he'll have to show
For all the years that he spent chasin'
This dream they call rodeo.
(To Chorus:)

STAND BY YOUR MAN

Words and Music by
TAMMY WYNETTE and
BILLY SHERRIL

You'll have __ bad times, and he'll have __ good times, doing __ things __ that you don't un - der - stand. ____

__ him, __ 'cause af - ter all, __ he's _ just a man. __

Chorus:

Cont. rhy. simile

Stand by your man. Give him _ two arms ____ to cling _ to and some - thing

Stand By Your Man – 3 – 2

Verse 2:
But if you love him, you'll forgive him.
Even though he's hard to understand.
And if you love him,
Oh, be proud of him,
'Cause after all, he's just a man.
(To Chorus:)

SOMETHING IN RED

Words and Music by
ANGELA KASET

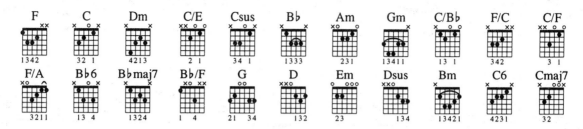

Slowly ♩. = 42

Intro:

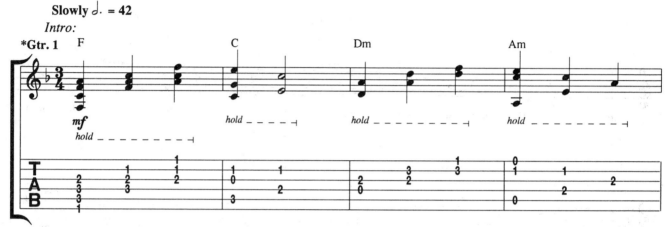

*Keyboard arr. for gtr.

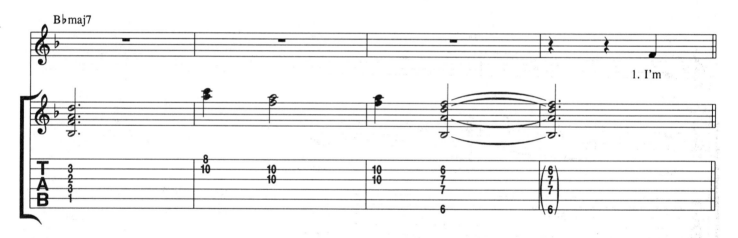

Verse:

look - ing   for ____   some - thing   in ____   red.

†Kybd. arr. for gtr.

Some - thing   that's ____   shock - ing   to   turn ____   some - one's ____   head.

Something in Red – 6 – 1

Something in Red – 6 – 3

Something in Red – 6 – 4

192

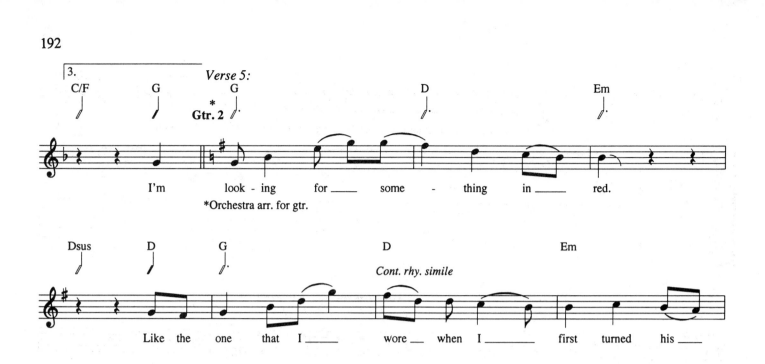

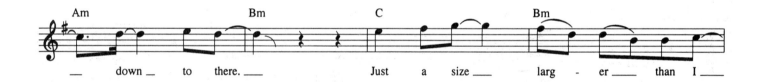

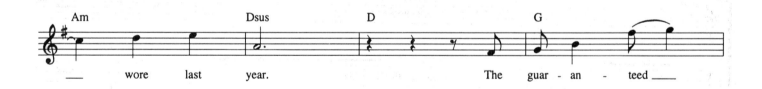

Something in Red – 6 – 5

gotta have ___ some-thing, I'm look-ing for ___ some-thing in

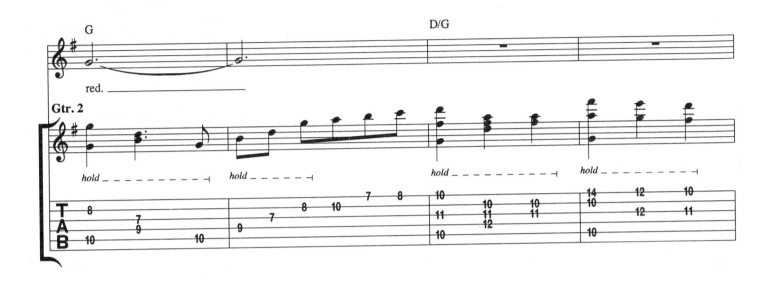

red. ___

Gtr. 2

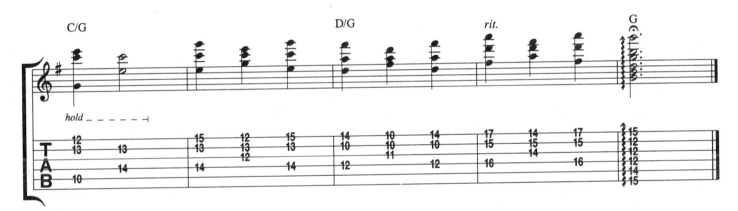

Verse 3:

I'm looking for something in white.
Something that shimmers
In soft candlelight.
Everyone calls us
The most perfect pair.
Should I wear the veil,
Or the rose in my hair?
Well, the train must be long,
And the waist must be tight.
I'm looking for something in white.

Verse 4:

I'm looking for something in blue.
Something real tiny,
The baby's brand new.
He has his father's
Nose and his chin.
We once were hot lovers,
Now we're more like friends.
Don't tell me that's just
What old, married folk do.
I'm looking for something in blue.

(To Verse 5:)

Something in Red – 6 – 6

THE RED STROKES

By
JAMES GARVER, LISA SANDERSON,
JENNY YATES and GARTH BROOKS

*Gtr. 2 ad lib. 2nd time.

The Red Strokes – 4 – 2

*Notes in parenthesis Gtr. 3 only.

Guitar Solo:

Cont. rhy. simile

Verse 2:
Steam on the windows, salt in a kiss.
Two hearts have never pounded like this.
Inspired by a vision
That they can't command.
Erasing the borders
With each brush of a hand.
(To Chorus 2:)

Chorus 3:
Oh, the red strokes, passions uncaged.
Thundering moments of tenderness rage.
Oh, the red strokes, fearlessly drawn.
Burning the night like dawn.
(To Coda)

STANDING OUTSIDE THE FIRE

By
JENNY YATES and GARTH BROOKS

Standing Outside the Fire – 4 – 1

Standing Outside the Fire – 4 – 2

Verse 2:
We call them strong.
Those who can face this world alone.
Who seem to get by on their own.
Those who will never take the fall.

We call them weak,
Who are unable to resist
The slightest chance of love might exist,
And for that forsake it all.

Bridge:
They're so hell bent on giving, walking a wire.
Convinced it's not living if you stand outside the fire.
(To Chorus:)

A THOUSAND MILES FROM NOWHERE

Words and Music by
DWIGHT YOAKAM

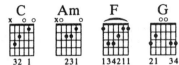

A Thousand Miles From Nowhere - 10 - 2

A Thousand Miles From Nowhere - 10 - 3

A Thousand Miles From Nowhere - 10 - 4

A Thousand Miles From Nowhere - 10 - 5

sand miles__ from no-where.

A Thousand Miles From Nowhere - 10 - 8

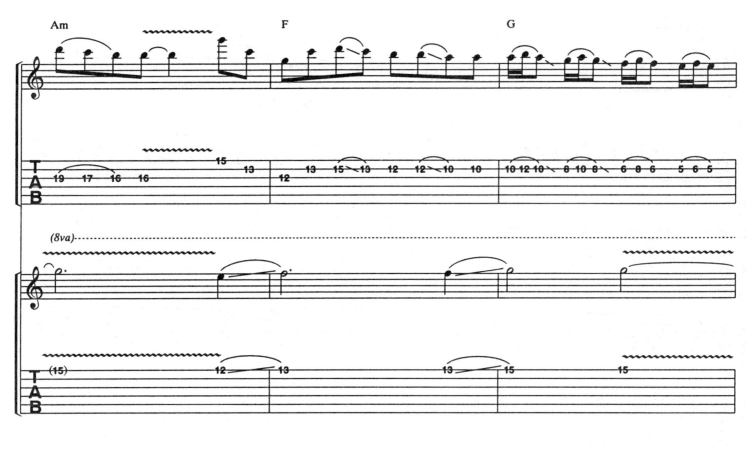

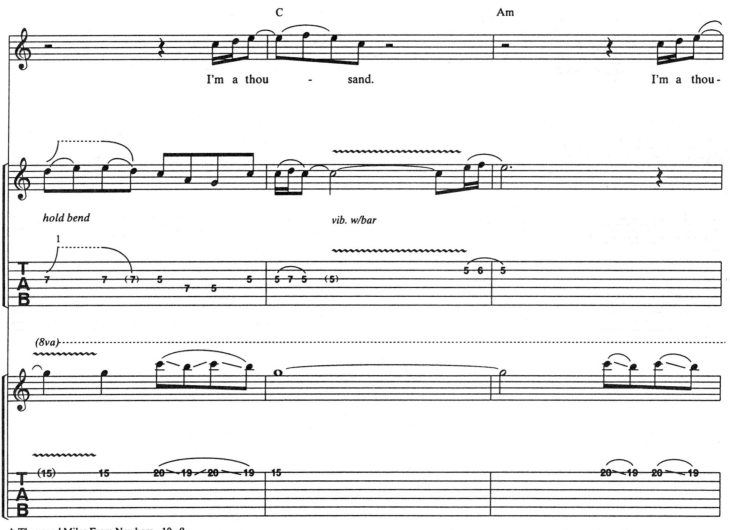

A Thousand Miles From Nowhere - 10 - 9

Verse 2:
I got bruises on my memory.
I got tear stains on my hands.
And in the mirror there's a vision
Of what used to be a man.
(To Chorus:)

TWO OF A KIND,
WORKIN' ON A FULL HOUSE

Words and Music by
DENNIS ROBBINS, BOBBY BOYD
and WARREN DALE HAYNES

Two of a Kind, Workin' on a Full House – 4 – 1

Two of a Kind Workin' on a Full House – 4 – 2

her lim - ou - sine. __ And her fa - vor - ite dress is her fad - ed blue jeans. __ She

loves me ten - der when the go - in' gets tough. __ Some - times __ we fight __ just so

Verses 3 & 4:
w/Rhy. Figs. 1 & 1A

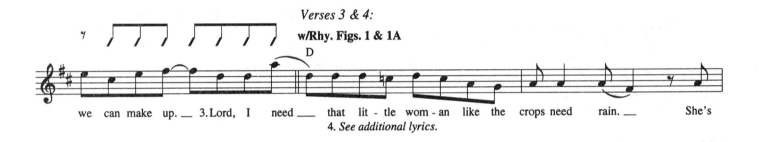

we can make up. __ 3. Lord, I need __ that lit - tle wom - an like the crops need rain. __ She's
4. *See additional lyrics.*

my hon - ey - comb and I'm her __ sug - ar cane. __ We real - ly fit to - geth - er if you

know what I'm talk - in' a - bout __ Yeah, we're

w/Rhy. Figs. 2 *(Gtr. 2)* **& 2A** *(Gtr. 1) Both 2 times*

two of a kind, __ work - in' on __ a full house.

This time __

Two of a Kind Workin' on a Full House – 4 – 3

Verse 2:
She wakes me every mornin'
With a smile and a kiss,
Her strong country lovin' is hard to resist.
She's my easy lovin' woman,
I'm her hard-workin' man, no doubt.
Yeah, we're two of a kind,
Workin' on a full house.
(To Chorus:)

Bridge 2:
This time I found a keeper, I made up my mind,
Lord, the perfect combination is her heart and mine.
The sky's the limit, no hill is too steep.
We're playin' for fun, but we're playin' for keeps.
(To Verse 3:)

Verse 4:
So draw the curtain, honey,
Turn the lights down low.
We'll find some country music on the radio.
I'm yours and you're mine.
Hey, that's what it's all about.
Yeah, we're two of a kind,
Workin' on a full house.
Lordy mama, we'll be two of a kind,
Workin' on a full house.
(To Coda)

Two of a Kind, Workin' on a Full House – 4 – 4

TWO PIÑA COLADAS

Words and Music by
SHAWN CAMP, BENITA HILL
and SANDY MASON

Two Piña Coladas – 7 – 1

UNANSWERED PRAYERS

Words and Music by
GARTH BROOKS, LARRY B. BASTIAN
and PAT ALGER

wife and I ran in - to ___ my old high school __ flame. And

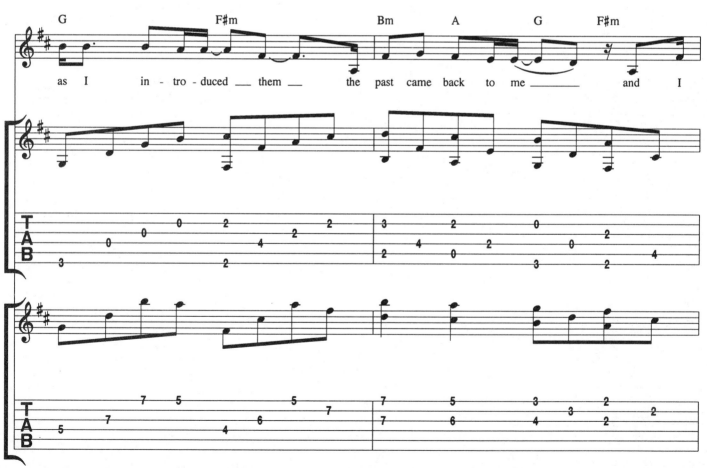

as I in - tro - duced ___ them ___ the past came back to me _____ and I

Unanswered Prayers – 5 – 2

(end Rhy. Fig. 2)

(end Rhy. Fig. 2A)

Verse 2:
w/Rhy. Figs. 2 & 2A *(1st 7 bars only)*
(w/Elec. gtr. fills)

2. She was the one ___ that I'd want-ed for all ___ times ___ and each night I'd spend pray-in' ___ that

God would make her ___ mine. And if He'd on-ly grant-ed me ___ this wish I'd wished back then. ___ I'd

Gtrs. 1 & 2

nev-er ask ___ for an-y-thing ___ a-gain. _____ Some-times I ___ thank

%. *Chorus:*
Rhy. Fig. 3

Gtr. 1

God ___ for un-an-swered prayers. ___ Re-mem-ber when you're talk-in' to the

Unanswered Prayers – 5 – 3

226

Unanswered Prayers – 5 – 4

* This acoustic gtr. part is gtrs. 1 & 2 arr. for one guitar.
Unanswered Prayers – 5 – 5

WE TELL OURSELVES

Words and Music by
CLINT BLACK and HAYDEN NICHOLAS

Fast ♩ = 92

Intro:

Gtr. 1
(Acoustic)

*Gtr. 2

*Tune ⑥ down to D

*Gtr. 3

*Gtr. 3 tab #'s in italics

Verse:

Rhy. Fig. 1

1. I ought-a know the look __ in an-oth-er's eyes, __ when there's some-thing on __ their mind. __
2. *See additional lyrics.*

(end Rhy. Fig. 1)

I

We Tell Ourselves – 5 – 1

*Several guitars arr. for one.

Verse 2:

I oughta know the language well,
I've heard me tell myself these things before.
I finally made my mind up,
My heart tells me to look for something more.
Determined not to wind up wondering
Was she the one, well, you never can be sure.

(To Chorus:)

WHICH BRIDGE TO CROSS
(Which Bridge to Burn)

Words and Music by
VINCE GILL and BILL ANDERSON

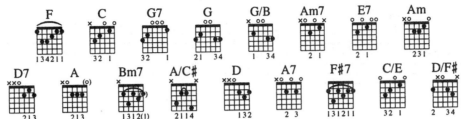

Tune down 1/2 step:

⑥= E♭ ③= G♭

⑤= A♭ ②= B♭

④= D♭ ①= E♭

Moderately slow ♩ = 86

Intro:

true love ___ and one that's brand _____ new. _____ I'm

C   F   C

not real-ly sure ___ that I know how ___ to

Gtr. 3 *(Electric w/clean tone)*

G(7)   C

love ___ one _____ and tell ___ one _____ we're ___ through. _____

Enter pedal steel

G/B   Am7

Chorus:
G

Enter fiddle
G7

*Gtrs. 1 & 2

I can't ___ sleep at _____ night.   I

Which Bridge to Cross (Which Bridge to Burn) – 5 – 2

*Gtr. 1 simile Gtr. 2 voicings to Fine.

*Pedal steel arr. for fingerstyle gtr.

Which Bridge to Cross (Which Bridge to Burn) – 5 – 3

Which Bridge to Cross (Which Bridge to Burn) – 5 – 4

Verse 2:
I knew this was wrong, I didn't listen,
'Cause a heart only knows what feels right.
Oh, I need to reach a decision
And get on with the rest of my life.

WHAT MIGHT HAVE BEEN

Written by
PORTER HOWELL, DWAYNE O'BRIEN
and BRADY SEALS

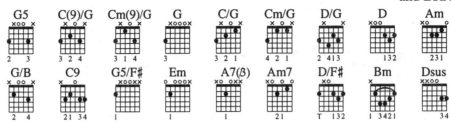

Slowly ♩ = 116
Half time feel throughout

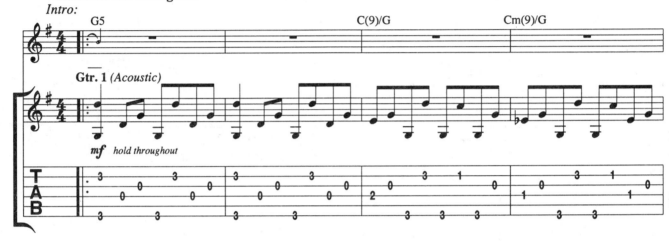

What Might Have Been – 4 – 1

What Might Have Been – 4 – 2

Verse 2:
We can sit and talk about this all night long,
And wonder why we didn't last.
Yes, they might be the best days we will ever know,
But we'll have to leave them in the past.
So try not to think about what might have been,
'Cause that was then, and we have taken different roads.
We can't go back again, there's no use giving in,
And there's no way to know what might have been.
(To Bridge:)

What Might Have Been – 4 – 4

WHAT THE COWGIRLS DO

By VINCE GILL
and REED NIELSEN

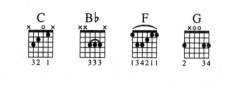

Gtr. 1 tuned down: (F6 tuning)
⑥ = C ③ = F
⑤ = F ② = A
④ = C ① = D

Moderately fast ♩ = 158

Intro:

*Gtr. 1 (Electric w/bright, clean tone)

*Gtr. 2 (Acoustic)

*Two gtrs. arranged for one gtr.

What the Cowgirls Do – 6 – 1

Coda

do. ____

Bkgd. vcl: What the cow-girls ____ do.

Well, _____ I love ____

Gtr. 1

w/Rhy. **Fig. 3** *(Gtrs. 1 & 3) simile*

____ it when they let their __ hair down

and dance __ real close to you. __

_____ And you know __ I'm a suck-er, ba - by, for what the cow-girls

Outro:
w/Rhy. **Fig. 1** *(All gtrs.) 2 times, simile to fade*

do. __

Bkgd. vcl: What the cow-girls __ do.

Of what the cow-girls do.

Of what the cow-girls __

Of what the cow-girls do. __

What the cow-girls __ do.

Of what the cow-girls

Play 4 times and fade

do.

What the cow-girls do. __

What those cow-girls

Verse 2:
They ain't no different up in Oklahoma,
They ain't afraid to stay up 'til dawn.
They love to cut a rug and chug-a-lug
Longnecks until their money's all gone.
(To Chorus:)

Verse 3:
Well, there's cowgirls all across the country,
From Baton Rouge to Bangor, Maine.
It ain't hard to see they'll be the death of me,
They're gonna drive my little heart insane.
(To Chorus:)

WHAT'S IT TO YOU

Words and Music by
CURTIS WRIGHT and
ROBERT ELLIS ORRALL

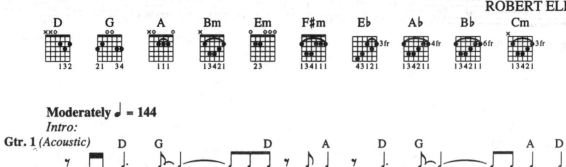

Moderately ♩ = 144

Intro:
Gtr. 1 *(Acoustic)*

Gtr. 2

Riff A

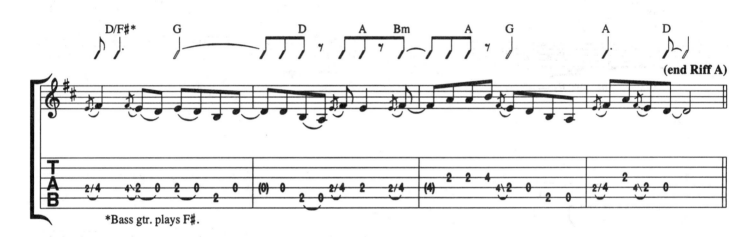

*Bass gtr. plays F♯.

(end Riff A)

Verse:

1. What's that? I __ hear an-gels sing-ing, tell-ing me __ to make my __ move. __
2. *See additional lyrics.*

Lis-ten to it, their voic-es ring-ing, ba-by. If you feel it, get in the groove. __

What's it to You – 4 – 1

Chorus:

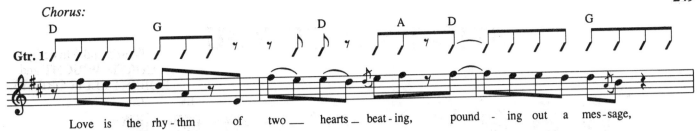

Love is the rhy-thm of two __ hearts __ beat-ing, pound - ing out a mes-sage,

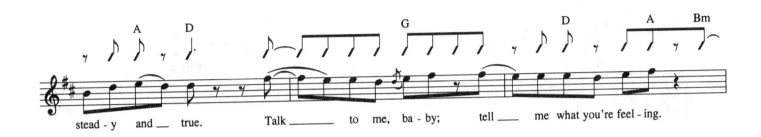

stead - y and __ true. Talk _____ to me, ba - by; tell __ me what you're feel - ing.

I know what love is; _____ what's it to __ you?

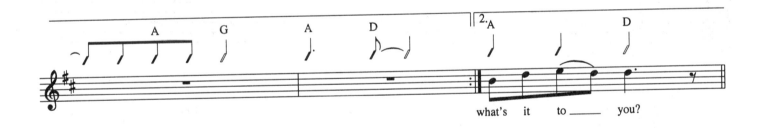

what's it to _____ you?

Guitar Solo:

What's it to You – 4 – 2

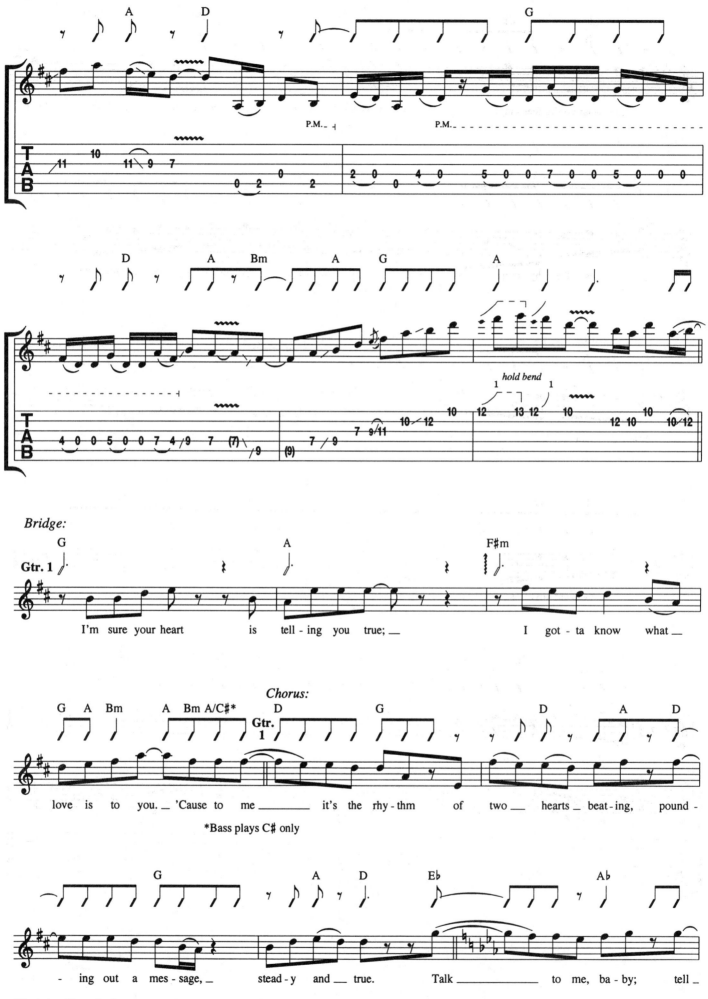

Bridge:

I'm sure your heart is tell-ing you true; — I got-ta know what —

Chorus:

love is to you. — 'Cause to me _____ it's the rhy-thm of two — hearts — beat-ing, pound-

*Bass plays C♯ only

- ing out a mes-sage, — stead-y and — true. Talk _____ to me, ba-by; tell —

me what you're feel-ing. I know what love is; — what's it to — you? Love —

_____ is the rhy-thm of two — hearts — beat-ing, pound-ing out a mes-sage,

stead-y and — true, Talk ____ to me, ba-by; tell ____ me what you're feel-ing.

I know what love is; — what's it to — you? I ____ know what love is; what's —

— it to — you?—

Verse 2:
Time's up;
Train's a-leavin', baby.
Are you ready
To take that ride?
Get on board;
Don't keep me waitin', baby.
Say you're willin' to cross that line.
(To Chorus:)

What's it to You – 4 – 4

YOUR LOVE AMAZES ME

Words and Music by
CHUCK JONES and AMANDA HUNT

Your Love Amazes Me – 4 – 1

Your Love Amazes Me – 4 – 2

Verse 2:

I've seen a sunset that would make you cry,
And colors of a rainbow reachin' cross the sky.
The moon in all its phases, but
Your love amazes me.

(To Chorus:)

GUITAR TAB GLOSSARY **

TABLATURE EXPLANATION

READING TABLATURE: Tablature illustrates the six strings of the guitar. Notes and chords are indicated by the placement of fret numbers on a given string(s).

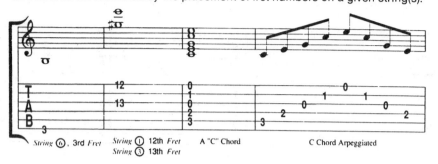

String ⑥ , 3rd Fret
String ① 12th Fret
String ③ 13th Fret
A "C" Chord
C Chord Arpeggiated

BENDING NOTES

HALF STEP: Play the note and bend string one half step.*

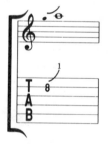

WHOLE STEP: Play the note and bend string one whole step.

PREBEND AND RELEASE: Bend the string, play it, then release to the original note.

RHYTHM SLASHES

STRUM INDICA-TIONS: Strum with indicated rhythm. The chord voicings are found on the first page of the transcription underneath the song title.

INDICATING SINGLE NOTES USING RHYTHM SLASHES: Very often single notes are incorporated into a rhythm part. The note name is indicated above the rhythm slash with a fret number and a string indication.

*A half step is the smallest interval in Western music; it is equal to one fret. A whole step equals two frets.

**By Kenn Chipkin and Aaron Stang

ARTICULATIONS

HAMMER ON: Play lower note, then "hammer on" to higher note with another finger. Only the first note is attacked.

PULL OFF: Play higher note, then "pull off" to lower note with another finger. Only the first note is attacked.

LEGATO SLIDE: Play note and slide to the following note. (Only first note is attacked).

PALM MUTE: The note or notes are muted by the palm of the pick hand by lightly touching the string(s) near the bridge.

ACCENT: Notes or chords are to be played with added emphasis.

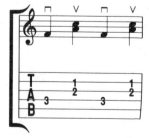

DOWN STROKES AND UPSTROKES: Notes or chords are to be played with either a downstroke (⊓ ·) or upstroke (∨) of the pick.